Classic American
Railroad Stations

Also by JULIAN CAVALIER:

American Castles
North American Railroad Stations

Classic American Railroad Stations

Julian Cavalier

The Tantivy Press

Classic American Railroad Stations text copyright ©1980 by
A. S. Barnes and Co., Inc.
San Diego, California 92121

The Tantivy Press
Magdalen House
136-148 Tooley Street
London, SE1 2TT, England

All rights reserved under International and Pan American Copyright Conventions.
No part of this book may be reproduced in any manner whatsoever without written permission from the publisher, except in the case of brief quotations embodied in reviews and articles.

First Edition

Manufactured in the United States of America
For information write to A. S. Barnes and Company, Inc.,
P.O. Box 3051, San Diego, CA 92038

Library of Congress Cataloging in Publication Data

Cavalier, Julian, 1931-
   Classic American railroad stations.

   Includes index.
   1. Railroads—United States—Stations—History.
I. Title.
HE1613.A15C38   725'.31'0973   78-69669
ISBN 0-498-02284-6

1 2 3 4 5 6 7 8 9   84 83 82 81 80

*This work is dedicated to the memory
of my beloved son Michael.
1957-1973*

Contents

Preface			9
Acknowledgments			11
Battle Creek, Michigan	1887-88	*Michigan Central*	15
Bethlehem, Pennsylvania	1873	*Central Railroad of New Jersey*	19
Branchville, South Carolina	1877	*Southern Railway*	23
Bryn Mawr, Pennsylvania	1869	*Pennsylvania Railroad*	27
Canaan, Connecticut	1872	*Housatonic & Connecticut Western*	31
Chatham, Massachusetts	1887	*Chatham Railroad*	35
Creston, Iowa	1899	*Chicago, Burlington & Quincy*	40
Dubuque, Iowa	1887-1944	*Illinois Central*	44
Durand, Michigan	1905	*Grand Trunk Railway*	48
Fort Payne, Alabama	1890-91	*Southern Railway*	55
Hamlet, North Carolina	1900	*Seaboard Air Line*	58
Howell, Michigan	1886	*Toledo, Ann Arbor & Northern*	63
Ida, Michigan	1875	*Lake Shore & Michigan Southern*	68
Ladson, South Carolina	1880s	*South Carolina Railway*	75
Lebanon, Pennsylvania	1885-1912	*Cornwall & Lebanon*	79
Liberty, Indiana	1902	*Baltimore & Ohio*	85
Lincoln, Nebraska	1892-93	*Chicago, Rock Island & Pacific*	90
Medford, Oregon	1911	*Southern Pacific*	94
Menlo Park, California	1867	*San Francisco & San Jose Railroad*	98
Mount Clemens, Michigan	1859	*Grand Trunk Railway*	103
Niles, Michigan	1891	*Michigan Southern*	108
North Conway, New Hampshire	1874	*Portsmouth, Great Falls & Conway*	114

North Easton, Massachusetts	1881	*Old Colony Railroad*	119
Oradell, New Jersey	1890	*New Jersey & New York Railroad*	123
Perris, California	1891	*Southern California Railway*	128
Pewee Valley, Kentucky	1867	*Louisville & Frankfort*	134
Point of Rocks, Maryland	1875	*Baltimore & Ohio*	138
Rockville, Maryland	1873	*Baltimore & Ohio*	143
Salem, Oregon	1896	*Southern Pacific*	146
San Juan Capistrano, California	1895	*Atchison, Topeka & Santa Fe*	150
Shawnee, Oklahoma	1902-03	*Atchison, Topeka & Santa Fe*	154
Somerville, New Jersey	1880s	*Central Railroad of New Jersey*	157
Stoughton, Massachusetts	1887-88	*Boston & Providence Railroad*	165
Strafford, Pennsylvania	1876	*Pennsylvania Railroad*	168
Timber, Oregon	1915	*Southern Pacific*	174
Vicksburg, Mississippi	1907	*Illinois Central*	181
Warren, Pennsylvania	1868-69	*Philadelphia & Erie*	187
Whitehall (Bryn Mawr), Pennsylvania	1859	*Philadelphia & Columbia*	193
Willits, California	1915-16	*Northwestern Pacific*	198
Ypsilanti, Michigan	1864	*Michigan Central*	205
Index			209

Preface

This work presents a series of capsule histories of a selected group of railroad station buildings located on the United States mainland. All of the stations presented have varying backgrounds, architectural styles and designs, and, in most cases, some measure of historic importance to the communities in which they are or were located. Emphasis is given to the architectural features of the buildings presented which are considered as being of primary importance, especially in view of the fact that such railroad station architecture has long since ceased to be built in America. These station buildings may also be considered, to some extent, as classic designs with respect to their architecture and the relatively short period that such buildings have come into being since the evolution of the railway system.

The station buildings have been selected for their various styles and designs and for their related historic interest. Some of them no longer exist, while others do and in varying conditions. Some have been fully restored while others have not, and some are still in active service while others are not. Whenever possible, both older and recent photographs are presented in order to show their past and more current states of existence, and in some cases to show varying degrees of alterations and revisions made to them over the years. Those that have been placed on the National Register of Historic Places, as of the time of this writing, are so indicated with the year of verification mentioned.

The purpose of this work is mainly to present a reasonable variety of railroad station designs based on the available data and to point out architectural features of the various styles, most of which date from the last half of the nineteenth century, as well as a few from the early twentieth century. In some cases the buildings have had drastic changes, while in others only minor changes have occurred.

It is hoped that this work may foster a new or better appreciation of the gradually diminishing styles of railroad station architecture in the United States. Fortunately, a small but growing number of railroad station buildings are being reused and preserved so that some fine examples of this architecture may remain for future generations to see and thus better understand its evolution. This understanding may also be extended to the buildings' role in the early development of the communities in which they existed, and perhaps a general idea may be acquired of that golden age of the railroad station.

J.C.

Acknowledgments

I wish to express my appreciation and thanks to the many individuals, historical societies, all the railroads that are represented here, the National Register of Historic Places, Historic American Building Survey, Historic American Engineering Record, State inventory, State Historic Preservation Plan, and numerous other institutions, for their kind attention and assistance to me when gathering material for this work.

Special thanks to:
George Kraus
John Uckley
William R. Main
Kenneth R. Jackson
William T. Wootton
Herbert H. Harwood, Jr.
Luther Folk
Donald T. Martin
Charles B. Castner
Robert Storks
Henry E. Bender, Jr.
David Oroszi
John P. Scharle

Warren B. Crater
Chas. Putnam
Samuel L. Breck, Jr.
A. S. Eggerton, Jr.
C. R. Davidson
R. A. Regalia
Thomas Kelcec

Also to:
Easton Historical Society
Historic Bethlehem Inc.
Chatham Railroad Museum
Branchville Railroad Shrine & Museum, Inc.
Connecticut Railroad Historical Association, Inc.
Warren County Historical Society
Orange Empire Railway Museum, Inc.
Montgomery County Historical Society
Nebraska State Historical Society
Menlo Park Chamber of Commerce
Massachusetts Bay Transportation Authority
Redwood Empire Assocation
And to all those whose photographs are presented in this work.

*Classic American
Railroad Stations*

Battle Creek, Michigan

The Michigan Central Railroad Company was, at one time, the largest and most successful railroad in the state of Michigan. It had served the town of Battle Creek, in Calhoun County since 1846 with a passenger depot on North Monroe Street. But the town had grown since then, and by the mid-1880s a new and larger updated station facility was needed for the nine thousand inhabitants of that manufacturing city. The railroad obtained the services of architects Rogers and McFarlane, of Detroit, who designed the new station for Battle Creek. Construction of the new station took place during 1887 and 1888, and on July 27, 1888, the handsome new station was opened for service to the public.

The station facility consisted of a main building with a large, imposing tower, and a smaller separate baggage express building. The station was built of red bricks, Lake Superior red sandstone trimmings, and covered with an Akron red-tiled roof. The main building, one and one-half stories high, is basically rectangular in shape, with a wide bay and twin semicircular end bays at each corner on the same side of the building, and is approximately 35 by 125 feet. The separate rectangular single story baggage express facility is about 50 by 25 feet and is located about 55 feet from one end of the main building.

The station has a hip roof whose wide overhangs are bracketed, with the two semicircular end bays having conical roofs. Dormers project high on the main roof and the large, square clock tower rises 72 feet above the main building in an almost central location on one side of the building. Window designs vary from broad-arched groups to individual double-hung, and narrow multigroups in the upper tower. At the Van Buren Street entrance is a porte cochere that gives access to one of the vestibules centrally located in the building.

The interior rooms originally consisted of large, ladies' and gentlemen's waiting rooms separated on either side of a short central hall that adjoined two small vestibules directly opposite each other on both sides of the building. A ticket office, toilets, and ladies' retiring room in one of the semicircular bays were also located on the first floor. The detached baggage express building contained a boiler room, lavatory, express office, and larger baggage room, both buildings being on the same exterior broad platform that surrounded them. A large fireplace was located at one end of the ladies' waiting room, with a broad chimney from it projecting a short distance above the roof peak line. The interior was antique-finished over quartered white oak with paneled wainscoting that all added to the spaciousness of the waiting rooms with their more than 16-foot-high ceilings.

BATTLE CREEK, MICHIGAN. A 1920 view of Battle Creek station showing the clock in place in the tower and the older, roof-style ridging. train-order signal, and darker painting scheme, all of which no longer exist. *Official Michigan Central Photo, courtesy of C.R. Davidson.*

BATTLE CREEK, MICHIGAN. An anonymous passenger waits for the train at Battle Creek station in April 1916. Note the single selective gate, at right in this view, that no longer exists. *John Uckley Collection.*

BATTLE CREEK, MICHIGAN. Originally built for the Michigan Central Railroad in 1887-88, the station has been used by the New York Central and Penn Central. The station was designed by Rogers & McFarlane, Architects of Detroit, Michigan, and still exists, as seen in this view of June 1974. It is currently used by Amtrak, and Penn Central uses part of the building for storage. *John Uckley.*

The luxuriant landscaping that completed the handsome setting of the station has long since gone. As the years passed, some alterations were made to the building that included the removal of the clock on the tower and the replacing of the original red-tiled roof with modern roofing material. An express office that had been attached to the station by a covered walk was rebuilt considerably.

The New York Central Railroad acquired the Michigan Central Railroad in 1918, and thus the Battle Creek station. Later, in 1968, the railroad was in turn acquired by the Penn Central Transportation Company which still

BATTLE CREEK, MICHIGAN. The glass-formed exterior ticket wicket on the first floor bottom of tower faces trackside and was still intact when this photo was taken in July 1974. *John Uckley.*

BATTLE CREEK, MICHIGAN. On the tower the faint outline in brick where the circular clock was once located can still be seen as shown in this 1974 view. *John Uckley.*

BATTLE CREEK, MICHIGAN. Looking down the line at Battle Creek station in July 1974. Note the eroding asphalt platform along track side. The station is still in use and has a ticket agent for Amtrak. *John Uckley.*

owns the Battle Creek station. In 1973 there was a fire in the station's tower that was believed to have been started by spontaneous combustion due to dust that had collected there over the years. The station is on the old New York Central double-track main line between Jackson, Michigan, and Chicago, Illinois, that was relocated through Three Rivers, Michigan, for New York Central freight trains into Elkhart, Indiana.

The only trains that now use this line are Amtrak passenger trains and local freights. The line change was made in 1961, and one track of the double-track line was torn out, except for passing tracks. The station again has a ticket agent representing Amtrak, and Penn Central uses part of the building for storage.

The Battle Creek station of the old Michigan Central Railroad is recognized by the Historic American Building Survey. It is also listed on the National Register of Historic Places, with verification dated 1971. The station, situated in downtown Battle Creek, is still an impressive structure and is a reminder of those days when passenger ease of travel and luxury were its foremost service to the public.

Bethlehem, Pennsylvania

The Bethlehem station was built in 1873 by the Central Railroad of New Jersey and is situated on the north bank of the Lehigh Canal, which is north of the Lehigh River in Pennsylvania. In the old days of rail operations, from twelve to fourteen trains stopped daily at the Bethlehem station located on the railroad's Lehigh and Susquehanna Division, commonly referred to then as the L&S. Teddy Roosevelt made a stop at this station in 1912 to talk from the rear observation car of the train before a large crowd of people who had gathered to listen to his campaign speech. This occasion was recorded and is shown in one of the photographs presented here.

The station is a fine example of Victorian-style railroad architecture in America. In its design it is basically rectangular in shape and symmetrical about the station's center. The two-story building has its long axis parallel to the tracks and is of red-brick construction with hexagonal, patterned shingles dominating most of the second-floor exterior walls. The central portion of the building projects slightly outward from the two narrow and short end wings. Above the windows of the first floor is a projected roof shelter skirting the building and supported by a series of large triangular-shaped braces. The window openings on the first floor are long and rectangular, with shallow arches above and low level concrete sills across the lower base. All windows are shallow arched on the top sash corresponding to the shallow arches, each sash having four glass panes except for the bay window areas. The doors also have glass light panels above them with shallow arches that blend well with the general design of the first-floor window styles.

BETHLEHEM, PENNSYLVANIA. The Bethlehem station looking east, September 1, 1951. Built by the Central Railroad of New Jersey in 1873, the station was still in active railroad service when this photo was taken. *Edward H. Weber.*

Immediately above the projected platform roof skirting is a series of twin brackets, spaced to support the slightly projected eaves. These ornate brackets are joined at their upper-half positions by a continuous, decorative, broad trim having a circular pattern series that continues around the building at both ends, ending at the twin brackets flanking the central area above the bay windows where the eaves discontinue. Dormer windows project slightly

BETHLEHEM, PENNSYLVANIA. Teddy Roosevelt made a stop at Bethlehem station in 1912 to deliver a campaign speech from the open platform of an observation car. A large crowd had gathered to see and hear him speak, as recorded in this view. *Courtesy of Historic Bethlehem, Inc.*

from the modest slope of the upper-floor, exterior-shingled walls in series of three on the central main block and one on the sides of the short, end wings in symmetrical pattern on the sides of the building. Each dormer has its own small, individual, roof projection with pairs of petite brackets flanking the deeper-arched windows found on this floor. The central upper portion above the first-floor, bay-window areas is continuous in brick construction with a pair of arched windows set deep and underlined by a single, continuous, concrete sill.

The roofs are at various levels, with the central portion dominating in its interesting design. This central portion projects on a axis at right angles to the main longitudinal axis, and the gabled end is hipped with ornate, decorative, patterned trimmings that are within the upper portions of this roof projecting out from the brick wall. Two brick chimneys top the building and are located on the ends of the roof sections that flank the central portion. It is believed that the second floor once contained living quarters for the station agent and his family, with station facilities occupying the first floor.

This railroad station has been designated by Historic Bethlehem, Inc. as a structure worthy of preservation. This idea took a positive direction in 1962 when the Central Railroad of New Jersey had agreed to lease the property to the Bethlehem Junior Chamber of Commerce rent free for twenty years, with a twenty-year renewal option. In the fall of 1962, the Bethlehem Jaycees announced plans to restore the old passenger station, thereby becoming the first organization to join Historic Bethlehem, Inc. in preserving a large area of the town's past.

BETHLEHEM, PENNSYLVANIA. Bethlehem station, looking west, November 22, 1970. The station had much restoration done by the Bethlehem Jaycees when this view was taken. *John P. Scharle.*

BETHLEHEM, PENNSYLVANIA. Number 107, the Harrisburger, west bound, at Bethlehem station in this view looking east on July 21, 1930. The upper portion of the station is seen at right just above the cars of this train that included a dining car and parlor car. *Harry Cotterell photo, courtesy of John P. Scharle.*

The project also provided for the use of the station building as a permanent meeting place for the Bethlehem Jaycees. Plans were approved by the general membership to include both exterior and interior restorations in a two-phased program of renovation that would restore it to its former character. The initial funds for expenditures rose from $12,500 to more than $50,000 as the project proceeded over the years. The first floor contains a museum, portraying authentic railroad artifacts creating the effect and mood that a nineteenth-century traveler would have experienced. The second floor contains redecorated meeting rooms and facilities for the Jaycees. Remodeling continues at this writing, and it is believed a restaurant, that will hopefully open in 1976, is to be located inside the station. The restoration program had also included repainting of the exterior to its original colors. Old paint was removed from trimmings, bracings, and other portions and repainted to its original three tones of brown or tan. Restoration of the exterior brick walls to their natural red color was also completed.

Small signs were hung from the ends of the platform skirting roof reading: Bethlehem Jaycees Terminal, signifying the current occupants of the restored building.

The Jaycees worked closely in conjunction with the Historic Bethlehem, Inc., and hoped other groups would be inspired by the station's restoration to undertake similar projects of restoring landmarks in the town. The Bethlehem section of the canal has also been restored and may now be used for leisure walking and picnicking.

The Bethlehem station is important as the foremost example of Victorian railroad station architecture in America and is a local landmark, symbolizing an era of growth in Bethlehem. The station is in excellent condition and continues to serve in its new role as the Bethlehem Jaycees headquarters, and platform areas are still used as a station stop for passengers by the railroad. The restoration of the station now shows it as it existed in 1873. This commendable project is certainly a credit to the city of Bethlehem.

Branchville, South Carolina

The Southern Railway station building at Branchville was built in 1877 by the South Carolina Railway and is located sixty-seven miles southeast of Columbia on the Columbia-Charleston main line in Orangeburg County, South Carolina. During a ten-year period from 1820 to 1830 the city of Charleston was in a position of economic decline and the need to establish trade with the upper Savannah region was realized. In order to bring farm products to the Charleston market from inland towns, the railroad, that would greatly help the economy of Charleston, was established. The railroad line from Charleston to Branchville was completed in 1832 by the South Carolina Railroad, and in 1833 it opened to Hamburg, to become the longest line in existence at that time. A few years later, in 1840, the line was extended with a branch line to Orangeburg, South Carolina creating a junction at Branchville.

In 1865, these rail lines were used by Confederate soldiers departing from Charleston. Union troops were diverted from Branchville upon learning of a battery in the area. That helped in preventing any potential destruction of the roadbed and junction point.

The new station building at Branchville was positioned on a site within the east wye intersection of the junction, so that tracks run generally on two sides of the building. The main line runs east-west, with the branch junction running north. The building itself is a single-story structure basically of brick construction with stucco finish on the exterior walls. The hip roof is new and covered with painted strip-layed tin roofing, and there are three chimneys, two from the waiting rooms and one from the dining room. Gabled-roof platform overhangs and gabled roof at one end are seen in one of the photo views taken when the station was in active railroad service. The windows are rectangular, double sash with multiglass panes in each sash. The dining room is separated from the waiting rooms and ticket office by a breezeway. Originally the platform area of the station had extended canopy sheds for passengers, but they were removed. Two bay windows are located on the building, one each facing the junction tracks on opposite sides.

The interior rooms include two waiting rooms, ticket office, rest rooms, dining room, kitchen, telegraph room, storage and baggage rooms. Remodeling had occurred in the fall of 1910 when another waiting room, the second such room, and exterior canopy sheds were added to the building by the Southern Railway.

BRANCHVILLE, SOUTH CAROLINA. Branchville station as it looked in 1917. Note that the 1910 additions of exterior platform sheds are seen here. These were later removed and, still later, reinstalled completely new by the current occupants of the station. Compare this view with the other restored station view taken at the same general position. *Branchville Historical Society Collection.*

BRANCHVILLE, SOUTH CAROLINA. Looking at the opposite end of the station from the previous view, showing some of the original overhang roofing, but shortened from the original that extended out further over the platform in the foreground. The station was in active railroad service when this shot was taken with trains on tracks at both sides of the building. *Courtesy of the Southern Railway System.*

BRANCHVILLE, SOUTH CAROLINA. A more recent view of the restored Branchville station, showing newly installed canopy sheds with the building in use as a transport museum of the Branchville Railroad Shrine & Museum, Inc. *Mike Knapik.*

BRANCHVILLE, SOUTH CAROLINA. A large, scale-model exhibit of the "Best Friend" locomotive on display in the Branchville station. Numerous other railroad artifacts are also on display throughout the building, now used as a transport museum. *Mike Knapik.*

The 1910 canopy-shed additions are those which were later removed by the railroad.

The last train run from the station was in 1962. Trains do not presently use the station as a station stop. Though the station is still owned by the Southern Railway Company, it is currently on a long-term lease acquired January 1, 1968, by the Branchville Railroad Shrine and Museum, Inc., which now occupies the building. Restoration of the station by the new occupants began in February 1968, and, having been restored both inside and out, it is now utilized as a transport museum. The dining room and kitchen have been restored to reflect the 1870-80s period. The front waiting room has numerous display posters and antique railroad artifacts, including a large scale model of the *Best Friend* locomotive. the central waiting room contains a model of the original station, as well as other railroad models related to railroad history, and there is a gift shop in this room. The telegraph room remains much the same as it originally was when in active service. The exterior platform canopy sheds were added in 1975 to reflect the original sheds, though they are slightly narrower in width, to allow for today's wider train loads passing the station. The station building was opened to the public in September 1969.

Branchville is also popular for its annual Raylrode-Daze festival in honor of the town's history. This event attracts thousands of people from throughout the southeast and greatly benefits the economy of the town. It also brings visitors to the restored Branchville station, where they can view the many fine displays on exhibit, purchase interesting items from the gift shop, and visit the handsome restaurant that serves meals on Sunday afternoons.

The Branchville station is important for its past role in the development of the town and its connection with several prominent visitors, including some past American Presidents who had stopped there. It is also believed to be the place of the world's oldest railroad junction established in 1840 when the line was extended from Branchville to Orangeburg in South Carolina. The Branchville station was placed on the National Register of Historic Places, with verification dated 1973, almost 100 years after it was built.

Bryn Mawr, Pennsylvania

The Bryn Mawr station was built in 1869 by the Pennsylvania Railroad and was located in the center of Bryn Mawr, a small suburban town in Montgomery County, Pennsylvania. The rail lines of the old Philadelphia and Columbia Railroad, which has been acquired by the Pennsylvania Railroad, ran in a curved route to the south of Bryn Mawr. In 1868 the rail lines were straightened out to eliminate the curved tracks and bring them through Bryn Mawr. This undertaking was completed in 1869, the same year the new Bryn Mawr station was erected to serve this new altered route.

Although the original working drawings of 1869 for the station are labeled as being from the Pennsylvania Railroad Construction Department, the station was believed originally designed by architect Joseph M. Wilson of the firm of Wilson Brothers and Company, who, in their 1885 *Catalog of Work Executed*, claimed the station though the firm was not established until 1876. However, Joseph M. Wilson was an employee of the Pennsylvania Railroad, and, it is believed, he designed the station building during that time prior to the founding of his firm. The drawings are also stamped with "Wilson Bros. & Co., Civil Engineers & Architects" on their reverse side.

The station site was at the northwest corner of Bryn Mawr and Morris Avenues, with the building facing northeast to the tracks and southeast to the street side, and eventually the station was fronted at trackside by a four-track main line of the railroad. In the early days of service, the station was the terminus for suburban passenger service to the city of Philadelphia. The building itself was a mid-nineteenth-century, Gothic-Revival style, one and one-half story with two-story sections, of an irregular plan but generally rectangular in shape, approximately 113 by 28 feet. The exterior walls were of irregular ashlar stonework that was most distinctive in overall appearance, especially with the varying window designs and roof styles. The windows were wooden sashes containing two-over-two lights with some one-over-one in pairs; most of the windows had stone hoods, while the attic and dormers had trefoil windows. The roofs consisted of gabled roofs with hipped ends and gabled-roof dormers with decorative eaves. The roofing was of slate and set with relief patterns. Originally the building had two sets of stone chimneys topped with a pair of octagonal stacks. One set of the chimneys was removed in 1900 during alterations. At trackside the entry porch was one bay wide covered with a flat roof and supported by paired columns with triple columns at the corners

BRYN MAWR, PENNSYLVANIA. An artist's view, showing a portion of the station scene at Bryn Mawr in 1875. Though the station was a busy place, this scene depicts a true rendering of life at the station over one hundred years ago as a train arrives along the long boardwalk-style platform as viewed from the upper portions of the pedestrian walk bridge. *Edwin P. Alexander Collection.*

BRYN MAWR, PENNSYLVANIA. A somewhat unclear but interesting view of Bryn Mawr station taken before open canopy sheds along the platforms were installed in the 1890s. The iron fencing separates through tracks at center with overhead, pedestrian walk bridge and station building seen at left in this early view. *Edwin P. Alexander Collection.*

BRYN MAWR, PENNSYLVANIA. An 1896 photo view of the Bryn Mawr station looking down the line with the station at left. Note that the open canopy sheds on both sides of the tracks had been installed at this time, and some carriages are parked waiting for passengers at extreme right. *Edwin P. Alexander Collection.*

as well as bracketing. In 1900 a lower bay was added at the east end. The west end had a plain two-bay-length porch with flat roof and wooden railings.

The interior of the station contained one-and-a-half-story-high waiting rooms in the east and center sections with a lavatory wing at the east end. The west end had two-story living quarters with three rooms on each floor and stairway to the upper floor, a porch, and a bathroom on the second floor over the porch.

The exterior area had landscaping and parking areas. Long, platform shelters were eventually added on both sides of the tracks in the mid-1890s, with a passenger shelter on the outer side of the tracks. A walkway was under the tracks, and near the station building was a cross-track pedestrian truss bridge with steps leading down to ground level on the outbound side and to the elevated station platform on the station side. A series of long-width steps fronting the station led down from the upper station platform to track level.

In the year 1900, the Pennsylvania Railroad made several major alterations to the Bryn Mawr station building. These included the lowering of the floor level in the east and central areas down to the track grade level with walls, doors, windows, and porches extended to accommodate this alteration. The baggage room was removed to allow for an increase in the floor space of the ladies' east-end waiting room. The east-end lavatories were revised, and the second floor lavatory over the west porch had been installed at this time. The ticket office was relocated from the bay window area to a corner of the waiting room. Some changes were also made to the living quarters, and, on the exterior, platforms and their shelters were extended.

The station continued in service until, with the general decline of passenger service, it was closed and eventually demolished in 1963. A smaller station-stop structure was put in its place. The old Bryn Mawr station was a most interesting and fine example of mid-nineteenth-century, suburban, Gothic-Revival style of railroad station architecture. It was also a unique structure of a design and style no longer being built in North America. It is interesting to note that the old Whitehall depot in Bryn Mawr, that this station had replaced, still is in excellent condition and is now used as a thrift shop.

Canaan, Connecticut

The Canaan Depot, also known as Union Depot, is located in Litchfield County in North Canaan, Connecticut. Although a small town, North Canaan was important as the junction of the Connecticut Western Railroad and the Housatonic Railroad. These two railroads were respectively known later as the Central New England, whose line ran from Hartford to Poughkeepsie, and the Berkshire Division of the New York, New Haven, and Hartford Railroad, now Penn Central.

The new Union Depot, built by the Housatonic and Connecticut Western Railroads, was completed on December 2, 1872. According to an old article printed December 6, 1872, in Canaan's newspaper, the *Connecticut Western News,* the depot "... was designed by Chief Engineer Shunk. The carpentry was under the supervision of G. H. Bundy of Lakeville, a general contractor, cabinetmaker, and maker of coffins. The masonry was done by Kilmer, of Canaan."

The Victorian style of the depot is not typical of the usual look of Victorian depots that were built at that time, but it is distinctive for its size and style. The town was very pleased with and proud of their new, grand Union depot, an elegant building, for it was indeed an outstanding structure in North Canaan. The building is basically of wood-frame construction with exterior walls of board and batten siding. Two long wings, each two stories high, are at right angles to each other and join to a three-story-high tower at the southwest corner at the intersection where the junction of the two railroad lines cross. Each of the wings is 90 feet in length and each was occupied by a different railroad facing its respective railroad lines. Both wings had spacious platforms with a wide, canopy-bracketed roof that runs continuously around the two tracksides of the building above the windows of the first floor. The distinctive tower had rooms for telegraph operators, and one can see for long distances from its octagonally shaped third floor that has windows on each wall face. The windows of the second and third floors are rounded-arched, similar to the styles of the double and single windows of the two second-floor wings.

All windows and doors have formed projected mouldings, those of the first floor being of a different style from those on the second-floor tower. The second-floor window mouldings arch down to a horizontal band moulding located three-quarters of the way up the windows. These create the effect of a continuous line of trim around the entire second floor. Below this trim line on the second floor the boards and battens are in vertical position, the same as on the first floor. Above the trim line of the second floor the boards and battens run horizontally, and the same is true of the third

CANAAN, CONNECTICUT. The Canaan station, also known as the Union Depot, is located in North Canaan, Connecticut, as seen in this view of April 23, 1967, taken prior to its repainting. The station was still in service at this time and until April 1971 when passenger service was discontinued but with freight service continuing until 1974. *Daniel A. Foley.*

CANAAN, CONNECTICUT. Looking at the inner angle of Canaan station at rear and opposite the junction point of the tracks directly beyond. Note the wide, raised platform at right and the protruding three-sided portion at the first floor where the wings join, as it looked in April 1967 when the station was still active. *Daniel A. Foley.*

CANAAN, CONNECTICUT. A July 1974 view of Canaan station in its repainted condition. The station appears in excellent condition, displaying its unique style of late-nineteenth-century Victorian design. The station is a State Historic Site and is on the National Register of Historic Places. *Herbert H. Harwood, Jr.*

story of the tower. The low-hipped roofs of the second-floor wings extend out slightly from the walls and are double-bracketed between the windows. The slightly projected tower roof is also bracketed but with more frequent spacing. This makes the roof line as neatly finished as the major roof lines. There are three brick chimneys, two on one wing and one on the other. Small circular windows are found on the ends of the first floor wings, and three-paned glass windows over the doors of the first floor are enclosed by arched mouldings.

Both stories have several rooms, and on the second story one of the larger rooms has a twenty-foot-long, semicircular counter for the once-used lunch room. Old, curved-back benches once occupied space on the platforms against the walls but have since been removed.

In April 1971 passenger service was discontinued; only freight service passed through Canaan until 1974 when that, too, was withdrawn. The interior was then closed except for a few rooms on the south side. A grain company also had rented some space in the depot. The depot was saved from possible demolition by a former Amtrak executive, Richard Snyder, who purchased it, and, thanks to him, the old depot exists today as a flourishing retail center and headquarters of the Connecticut Railroad Historical Association which succeeded in obtaining state and county recognition of the depot building. The Association also supports railroads, seeks to revive the old Housatonic route, and maintains a Caboose Museum and Station Museum.

The Canaan depot is important for its role in the early development of the town and as a junction point in earlier times when the two railroads passed through it. The depot's architecture is significant in its unique style of late-nineteenth-century, Victorian-style railroad depot design. The Canaan Depot was placed on the National Register of Historic Places, with verification dated 1972, and is also a State Historic Site.

Chatham, Massachusetts

When the first stage coach entered the small town of Chatham, Massachusetts, in 1814, it drew the attention of the entire population. It was not until February 3, 1863, that the first of a long series of actions by the townspeople, in regard to rail service, was taken. As the years passed, issues and proposals were taken up and discarded numerous times until early 1887 when a company was formed and called the Chatham Railroad Company. The company was made up mainly of Chatham stockholders and headed by the Honorable Marcellus Eldredge as President and Charles Bassett as Clerk and Treasurer.

At nine o'clock on the morning of May 24, 1887, the President of the company pierced the soil with a shining new shovel that marked the turning of the first sod for the railroad. These opening ceremonies were attended by more than one hundred men, women, and children, all of whom followed the action of the President using the new shovel that had been purchased to mark the beginning of the grading for the line that would run from Harwick to Chatham. As the ceremonies proceeded, a small string of cart teams began to arrive, moving slowly along the dusty road in the distance. These were the Italian laborers who were to grade the line route from Chatham and level the large mounds of earth where the track was to be located.

When the graders were finally finished with their job, railroad ties that had been cut in the swamps of Maine were transported to the site. Rails were laid by Old Colonial Railroad employees, with ties being carted to advanced positions by night crews. It is not known by whom or where the golden spike was driven in the first-laid track, but the work progressed with one mile of track laid per day until it was finally completed.

Buildings, including an engine house, a turntable, a car house, a building for tools and hand cars, and a handsome depot, were also constructed. The Chatham depot was built between May and November 1887 of wood frame construction with clapboard exterior measuring overall 45 by 21 feet. It was a one-story building with an elegant two-story centrally located tower at trackside. The interior contained the main waiting room, and there was a ticket agent's office in the first floor tower area. The waiting room that occupied most of the floor space had a 12-foot-high ceiling. There were two stoves for heating, one in the waiting room and the other in the adjoining ticket office. The depot was finished with ornamental trimmings on the exterior. The outside walls were originally painted a light, drab color with about a 3-foot-high base painted in dark red, like the trimmings. The roof of the main building and conical tower was a chocolate red and

CHATHAM, MASSACHUSETTS. The Chatham depot as it looked about 1890, just a few years after it was built, showing its original construction. Note the date and name just above the bay window, reading: Chatham—1887. *Courtesy of Eleanor Henderson.*

could be clearly seen from most places in the town at that time. The depot faced north, and when completed looked much like an Oriental pagoda, very pleasing to the eye and certainly a credit to the small town of Chatham.

Large signs reading "look out for the eingine" were placed nearby, and telegraph poles were erected along the line to the depot to complete the picture. The first station master was Augustus L. Hardy, and Mathias Slavin was engineer. All was ready for the big event as the railroad opened for traffic on November 22, 1887, a day that had been anticipated for more than twenty years.

The first carload of freight consisted of cranberries that were shipped from Chatham to Chicago. It was a grand carnival day for the town, with free rides from Chatham to Harwick; many rode the trains all day back and forth along the line. The noon train of six cars was filled with an estimate of over seven hundred passengers. Some even rode the freight train that came through from Harwick in twelve minutes. Passengers boarded and departed at Chatham, South Chatham, where another depot had been built, South Harwick, Harwick, and Harwick Center. The celebrations carried on into the evening hours, as this was one of the most important events in the history of Chatham.

The really big celebration of the railroad was on the following July 4, 1888. It was a day of parades, speeches, dinners, and fireworks. One of the displays spelled out in colors, "Chatham Railroad Co." An estimated 1,600 passengers rode the line to Chatham for the celebration.

The railroad continued to prosper with passenger and freight service. Fares from Harwick to Chatham were thirty-five cents, and freight from the same points was 50 cents per hundred pounds. Two years later another depot was opened in West Chatham, and in 1891 more than 23,000 passengers had been carried on the Chatham Railroad line. As the years passed, the Chatham depot was always a busy place with passenger, freight, and railway express service.

The line was later leased for ninety-nine years to the New York, New Haven and Hartford Railroad, and the business continued. In 1925 rumors had begun to spread through the town that the N.Y. N.H. & H. intended to discontinue operations on the line. As the rumor persisted, passenger trains stopped suddenly, and a gasoline bus, which the town called the "Toonerville Trolley," was put on to replace it, though freight trains continued in service. In 1927 a town meeting with the railroad officials was held to discuss better service to this part of Cape Cod, but the railroad's promise to report on it came to nothing. By 1930 service amounted to only two trips a day, and it seemed the railroad wanted to eliminate passenger service altogether, though it was clearly stated that the leasee was to provide adequate passenger service, for which there was no lack of passengers at the time. The N.Y. N.H. & H. then announced that it would halt all rail passenger service to Chatham and that the gasoline bus would be taken off and replaced by bus service provided by the New England Transportation Company. The town residents were much concerned over the halting of the rail passenger service which was considered a public necessity and convenience, required under the lease. Protests were lodged with the Department of Public Utilities and the

CHATHAM, MASSACHUSETTS. Chatham depot as it looked in 1910. Note the differences in the bay trimmings and painting arrangement as compared to the 1890 photo view. The wood platform remains comparable, and the automobile has now come into view, as have the telegraph poles. *Courtesy of Charles W. Cartwright.*

CHATHAM, MASSACHUSETTS. A rear view of the Chatham depot as it looked in April 1975 as the Chatham Railroad Museum. The wide open spaces around the depot have long been filled in with dwellings, but the depot remains basically the same in its architecture. *Edward Hunt Photo, Collection of Herber H. Harwood, Jr.*

matter taken up with New Haven officials. There were many more meetings but all to no avail. The last agent of the Chatham depot, Herbert Moran, received orders to close the depot on July 5, 1930. It was not a justified action by the railroad. The townspeople realized that this depot had done more business than any of the others, and they felt the railroad had not kept faith with them. It was evident that all rail service would soon end for the town of Chatham, which was the last to be reached by railroad service and now the first from which it was retracting.

No special ceremony was held in 1937 as the last freight train rolled into Chatham with one car of assorted goods and rolled out again, marking the end of fifty years of rail activity at Chatham. Rolling stock, rails, and ties were sold, with the proceeds distributed among the town's stockholders who had lost their investment. The 7.8 miles of track from Chatham to Harwick took workmen a month to dismantle. The elegant little Chatham depot was now a lone sentinel and reminder of happier times when rail service activity once abounded at its doors.

The depot stood idle until 1956 when a public-spirited woman in Cleveland, of Chatham heritage, provided for its maintenance by means of a trust. In 1960 Mr. Frank Love, a retired New York Central official and true railroad buff, came to Chatham in retirement and created the Chatham Railroad Museum out of the old depot. The depot was painted, preserved, and made a focal point for Chatham. Mr. Love, who also directed the museum at that time, was able to obtain from older families of Chatham some original artifacts of the railroad that had passed from the scene twenty-three years prior to the opening of the museum in 1960. Mr. Love passed away on January 27, 1975, a sad day for Chatham. He had served as director from the time the museum opened until November 1974, when Mr. William R. Main succeeded him as director.

The old Chatham depot, now known as the Chatham Railroad Museum, opened on July 27, 1960. It currently exists in excellent condition and is opened to the public during the summer vacation months of July and August. In addition to the numerous interesting displays that visitors can see, color postcards and history of the Chatham Railroad are on sale. In 1974 4,054 visitors were counted and the 15-year total of visitors to that time was 87,450. A visit to the old Chatham depot is a rewarding experience where one can imagine those days in 1887 when the entire town rejoiced with the opening of the little, and still elegant, Chatham Railroad depot.

Creston, Iowa

Creston station is located in Union County, Iowa, 393 miles west of Chicago, Illinois, on the Chicago to Omaha, east-west Burlington Route main line in the central part of the state. The station was built in 1899 by the Chicago, Burlington and Quincy Railroad, now Burlington Northern, at a cost of $75,000, and was the largest and finest station building constructed in Iowa at that time. Creston was an important railroad center, and the large two-and-one-half-story station was a division point, with all business for southwest Iowa regulated from this building. In addition to the station building, the area contained the Creston rail yards, two branch lines, and the Creston roundhouse, the largest of its kind of the C. B. & O. system. One foreign railroad also had a line originating at Creston that was controlled from the Creston station. Being a division headquarters, the station building housed, in addition to passenger facilities, offices of the train master for yard traffic and forming up of trains, and the master carpenter, who was in charge of all section and bridge work for the entire division, as well as other offices pertaining to railroad duties.

In the early period of its existence, the Creston station was an imposing building distinctly visible from Iowa's prairie, and an important busy center of the town. The building is constructed of pressed yellow brick with a cut stone base around the building that rises to the first-floor window sills and is approximately 43 by 173 feet in plan with a 53-foot overall height. A broad, brick sidewalk surrounds the building, with a small automobile parking facility for express office customers on the northeast corner. The roof is of red tile, with copper cornice at its base where it joins the walls. There is a total of six large dormers, two on each side and one at each end, all of similar size and design. The main block of the building is two and one-half stories, with a one-and-one-half-story wing that has a single, brick chimney centrally located on its lower crested roof peak.

The architectural design is generally symmetrical about its long axis. Windows and doors of the first floor are all arched and are bordered in brick trim down to the stone base. The large windows of the second floor of the main block, and those of the dormers, are of a rectangular design, with those of the dormers being narrower. Narrow stone courses suround the building above the first-floor windows and doors, the upper course forming the sills of the second-floor windows of the main block.

The several rooms occupying the first floor consist of a large, general waiting room, ticket office, check room, baggage room, two rest rooms, and a lunch counter. A central corridor off the waiting room runs through the first floor to the east-end baggage room and separates the smaller rooms, with the ticket office and the lunch counter on one side, rest rooms and large storage room on the other side. The waiting

CRESTON, IOWA. An early view of Creston station when it was in active railroad service and was a major center of operations. With its yellow brickwork and red-tiled roof, the building was an imposing structure and remains a Creston landmark today. *Creston News Advertiser, courtesy Union County Historical Society.*

CRESTON, IOWA. This east view shows Creston station as it looked on December 5, 1967, when the building was still occupied. It had been in service since 1899, the year it was built. *William F. Rapp, Jr.*

CRESTON, IOWA. A west view of Creston station taken December 1967. Still in use at this time, the building was eventually inactivated but placed on the National Register of Historic Places in 1973. *William F. Rapp, Jr.*

room is well designed with attractive color patterns. The walls are of white ceramic brick and match four large, round pillars that support natural-oak beams of the inlayed ceiling. The floors are of dark red marble for contrast, and solid-oak benches in their natural finish still remain in place.

A stairway at one end of the corridor leads to the second floor and a long central hallway that ends at a large telegraph office. On either side of the hallway are several offices of local officials, dispatcher, road master, division superintendent, conductors, physician, and others. A small stairway at the east end of the hall leads to the upper story area composed of two large rooms, one now a store room, the other being used for schooling sessions.

The two 1967 photo views illustrated here show the station when occupied, but it has since been inactivated. Some moderate deterioration has taken place in the building; some windows are broken; paint is scaling off; and the interior is in need of attention. However, the building is structurally sound and has withstood the elements of weather for over three quarters of a century.

The station is a unique landmark for Creston in its design and size, as no other building has since been erected in that area to compare with it. It is also important for its role in the development of the area and as a one time major railroad center in Creston, as well as being in a style of railroad station architecture no longer being built. The Creston station was placed on the National Register of Historic Places, with verification dated 1973.

Dubuque, Iowa

The Dubuque station is located in Dubuque County, Iowa, 182 miles west of Chicago on the Illinois Central Gulf's Chicago to Sioux City main line, and just west of the Mississippi River. Dubuque is also the intersection of the three state lines of Iowa, Wisconsin, and Illinois. The original large main station of the railroad in Dubuque was built in 1887 by the Illinois Central Railroad, now called the Illinois Central Gulf Railroad, due to a merger with the Gulf, Mobile & Ohio Railroad in 1972. The station as originally built was a two-and-one-half-story brick building with a high ornate tower at one end that rose well above the main building. This station has since undergone one of the most drastic changes in its design so that it is no longer recognizable as it originally existed, and one might consider that the existing station building at Dubuque now is an entirely new structure.

The original main building was a magnificent structure generally rectangular in plan, about 60 by 170 feet with the tower rising 145 feet overall. Almost all the doors and windows of the first floor were arched and had alternate colored voussoirs, except for those few at the south end. The second-floor windows were rectangular, and all dormer windows were arched with the same voussoir patterns as those of the first floor. The large, square tower at the north end was almost reminiscent of a cathedral tower and no less elegant in its design. There were two main gabled bays that projected out slightly from the main block of the building and they, along with the dormer gabled roofs and main roof peaks, all had ornate ridging of identical design. The red bricks of the building were in contrast to a series of horizontal, light-colored, stone courses that surrounded the tower and main building. The lower floor contained passenger station facilities, and the upper floors were believed to contain offices for various railroad duties. A walkway surrounded the building, and a long platform canopy was at trackside during the period of the station's existence prior to alterations.

In March 1944 the Illinois Central Railroad's Office of Engineer of Buildings had major alteration plans drawn up that would virtually wipe out any resemblance to the original Dubuque station building's physical appearance. In fact, the building that exists now at Dubuque is practically all new construction. Notes on the 1944 drawings in regard to removal and alterations to the station building call for removal of the entire canopy at trackside; removal of the entire tower and other large portions of the building, notably the entire second and third floors; removal of the balance of the building down to the top of the foundations, except for certain portions of interior crosswalls and portions of other exterior walls; removal of the entire first-floor construction, with the hole under floor level to

DUBUQUE, IOWA. The Dubuque passsenger station as it originally existed is seen in this view taken shortly after it was built in 1887. This grand structure of red brick and contrasting bands of light-stone courses no longer exists today. Note the covered platform at left and the unpaved road area at right. *Courtesy Illinois Central Gulf Railroad.*

be filled with sand for areas required; and the remaining portions to be left in place. An entire 36-foot section, 52 feet in from a south-end annex was completely removed, slicing the structure and separating it into two parts, the shorter south end part eventually to become a detached annex but almost completely rebuilt. The drawings indicated those portions of the original building that were to remain so that reference to entire removals refer to areas indicated on the drawing.

With the above alterations completed, the plans for the new Dubuque station building showed a single-story building with almost the same floor space area of the first floor that consisted of a large main building and a smaller detached annex at the south end, both on the same site of the original building. The main new building portion is about 62 feet wide by 170 feet long, begins at the same point where the inside tower wall had joined to the original main building wall, and extends south 170 feet. A 40-foot open space, the area that had been sliced separating the original structure in two, separates the main building from the new annex that extends south another 48 by 31 feet. Reconstruction of both structures used salvaged brick except for the wall facings, which is of new Sioux City common red brick, with precast concrete trim for base, sills, and coping. New flat roof design, partitions, and other framing made use of salvaged materials along

DUBUQUE, IOWA. This view was taken in the mid-1940s shortly after the 1944 revisions and rebuilding. In comparison with a similar view taken in 1967, none of the trackside doors are bricked in and no roof-pole platform lighting lamps had been installed. Tracks are clear of weeds, showing the new concrete platform clearly, windows and doors are painted a darker color, and a large chimney is clearly visible at left in this view. *Courtesy Illinois Central Gulf Railroad.*

DUBUQUE, IOWA. A comparable view of the station taken July 6, 1967, showing the alterations as compared to the mid-1940s view. *William F. Rapp, Jr.*

with new materials, such as sheet-metal work, composite roofing, and millwork. New platforms were installed and extended north and south, older portions were repaired, and the old coal track siding at the southwest side was moved, extended, and provided with a bumper.

In general, the new, revised, station building was made into a modern structure, with limited passenger facilities at the north end approximately 62 by 50 feet in floor area. The entire balance of the main building includes a combined baggage and mail room, and a large central railway express agency with combined wareroom. At the south end is a group of smaller rooms containing rest rooms for trainmen having short layovers, a report room with lockers, toilet rooms, supervisor of track room, and a water chemist's room.

The small, annex building contains a heater room with a new brick chimney, an adjoining coal room, a car-knockers supply room, a small, switchman's room, and an equally small, special agent's room. New-modern-styled windows were installed throughout both buildings. Some additional revisions were made during the year of 1944, but these were of a minor nature.

Amtrak runs one passenger train per day each way between Dubuque and Chicago. There is an Amtrak ticket office now in the waiting room of the station. The existing Dubuque station building is used today by the Illinois Central Gulf Railroad, mainly as a freight office, and well illustrates the drastic changes that have taken place in regard to rail passenger travel in the United States this century.

Durand, Michigan

Durand station, located in Shiawassee County, 66.9 miles northwest of Detroit, Michigan, was built in 1905 by the Grand Trunk Railway Company of Canada. During the town's major growth period from 1887 to 1905, Durand's population increased from 250 to 3,000, and it became one of the busiest railroad towns in the state. Thirty-five passenger, nine local, and over one hundred freight trains passed through Durand daily in 1904. In 1905, when the station was erected, it served the Grand Trunk Western, the Toledo, Ann Arbor, and Northern Michigan Railway. At some point after 1905, the Toledo, Ann Arbor, and Northern

DURAND, MICHIGAN. Grand Trunk locomotive No. 5041 stopped at Durand station on October 10, 1938. Note the darker color of the trim and window framing. The roof dormers were eventually removed. *George B. MacKay Collection.*

DURAND, MICHIGAN. A Grand Trunk Western passenger train stopped at Durand station on June 4, 1961. The station looks much the same in this view as it did when originally built in 1905. *Howard W. Ameling Collection.*

Michigan Railway became the Ann Arbor Railroad, which is now part of the Penn Central.

In 1904, the Ann Arbor Railroad relocated its main headquarters in nearby Owosso, but left the ticket office and freight facilities at Durand. The Ann Arbor's original buildings were torn down after space for the railroad was provided in the new Durand station in 1905. By 1911, the Grand Trunk Railway Company had employed 50 percent of Durand's population.

Durand station was very similar to its predecessor. The earlier station was destroyed by fire on the night of April 16, 1905, only two years after it was built. The new Durand station, designed by Spier and Rohns, architects of Detroit, was erected by the same contractor. Only six months after the fire, on October 17, 1905, the new station was completed. The only major difference in the two stations is that the roof detailing was simplified on the newer station.

The basic structure is two and a half stories, 244 feet long by almost 50 feet wide. Two of the main features are the extended, overhang porch and symmetrical, conical roofs over rounded bays at the north end of the building. An eight-foot-wide overhang around the building, forming a sheltered porch, is supported by a series of metal brackets. The southern portion of the building is one and one-half-stories high with

DURAND, MICHIGAN. Durand station in 1974, showing the roof dormers removed and new roofing on the entire structure. *John Uckley.*

DURAND, MICHIGAN. A front left view of Durand station, showing tracks that still existed on both sides of the building. *Courtesy Grand Trunk Western*

DURAND, MICHIGAN. A side-view portion of Durand station during the winter of 1974. The building is basically of the same design on both sides, except for the window and door variations in location. *John Uckley.*

DURAND, MICHIGAN. A general rear view of Durand station in 1974, showing the baggage-section area and the single dormer that remains. *John Uckley.*

DURAND, MICHIGAN. Looking down one of the main lines fronting Durand station in the summer of 1974. The station has been restored with new painting and other renovations. *John Uckley.*

two brick chimneys. The building is of brick construction with cut stone about four feet up from the base.

The building originally had a tiled roof and four dormer windows on each side. These were removed in 1965 when asphalt roofing replaced the tile roofing. Dormer-type windows still exist at both ends of the structure, though old drawings still show the original dormer windows.

The first floor interior has 12-foot-high ceilings with the second-floor ceilings at 10 feet. Originally, the first-floor rooms consisted of a main waiting room at the north end, a centrally located dining room, kitchen, mail room, and express room at the south end. An open east-west passageway separated the extreme south-end baggage room on the first floor. The second floor consisted mainly of offices.

As rail passenger service declined over the years, the Ann Arbor tracks were eventually taken up, but all other tracks still remain. Passenger service at Durand had ceased for three years until the inception of Amtrak in May 1971. The railroad considered demolition of the station, but in 1974 negotiations between the Grand Trunk Western and the City of Durand resulted in an agreement that the cost of renovating and maintaining the large station would be considerable for the small community. The Durand Area Bicentennial Commission instituted a broad, public-pledge campaign to find out whether there was enough financial support and public interest to lease and maintain the station for a restaurant, museum, shops, offices, and as a passenger stop for the Amtrak Chicago-Port Huron train.

Public interest did take its positive effect.

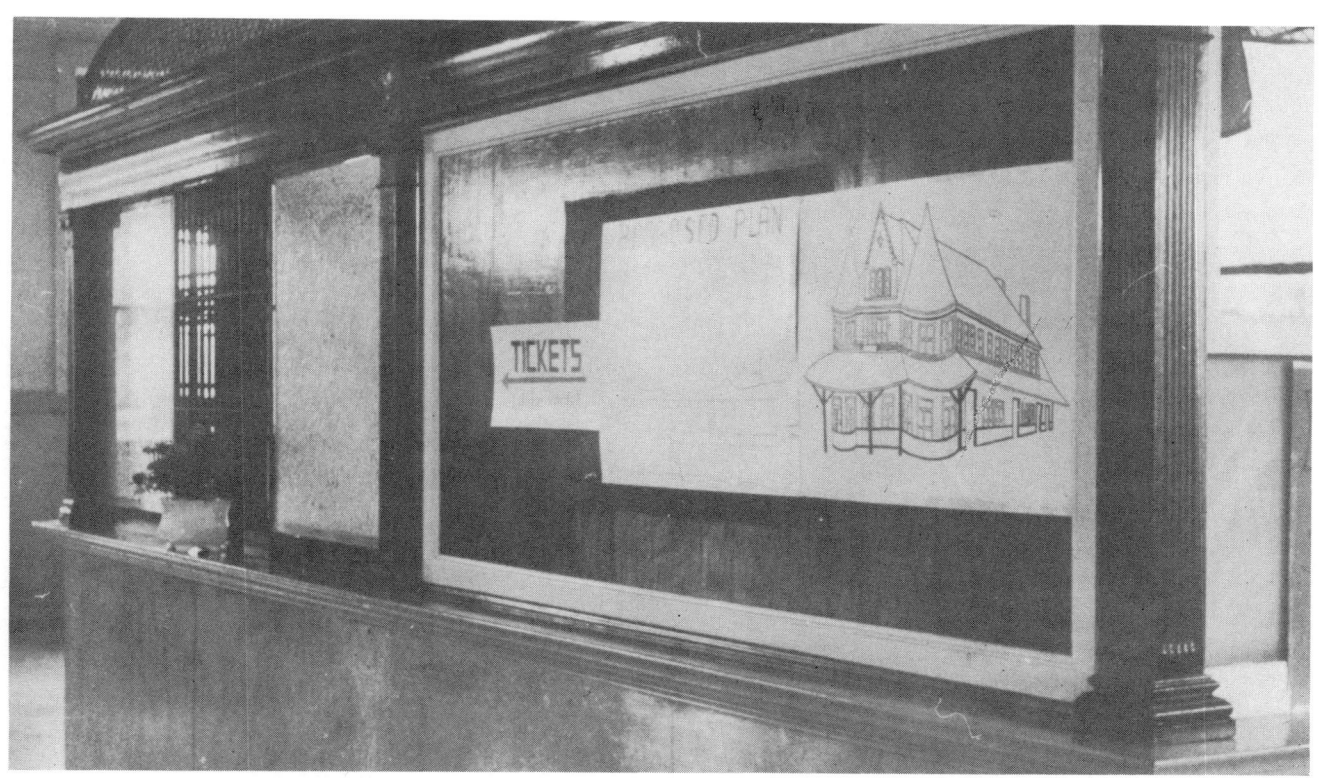

DURAND, MICHIGAN. An interior view of the ticket wicket, with drawings posted showing plans for leasing portions of the building for other uses. *John Uckley.*

DURAND, MICHIGAN. A 1974 interior view of the ticket wicket and portions of columns. Note the screen covering over the wicket. *John Uckley.*

DURAND, MICHIGAN. At the inagural run of Amtrak's new "Blue Water" on the Port Huron to Chicago line, with crowds of rail fans greeting its arrival on September 15, 1974. A portion of the station is seen at left. *John Uckley.*

The station was renovated to some degree, with much public assistance, and the expected return of rail passenger service on September 15, 1974 generated new enthusiasm in the old railroad town, as workmen added a new platform for the coming service. On September 13, 1974, the inaugural run of Amtrak's new *Blue Water* took place with crowds of townspeople and rail fans there to meet the train.

In early 1971, the Durand station was placed on the National Register of Historic Places. The station still exists and is in good condition and structurally sound. Though the return of limited passenger service now exists at Durand, the "golden age" of passenger travel to Durand has long passed. But, with the return of this service, Durand continues to be a center of railroad activity, and the grand station remains as a reminder of those days when as many as forty-two passenger trains ran daily in and out of Durand.

BETHLEHEM, PENNSYLVANIA. The Bethlehem station as it looked on a winter day, January 7, 1975. The former Central Railroad of New Jersey station has been restored by the Bethlehem Jaycee's and used as their headquarters. Today, the station looks much the same as it did when built in 1873. *John P. Scharle.*

DURAND, MICHIGAN. Built in 1905, the Durand Station was still in active use when this view was taken on April 5, 1975, a few days after a snow storm in the area. This is the second station on the site; the first was destroyed by fire on April 16, 1905. It is a remarkable feat that the new station was built and ready for service that same year, especially considering its size and the clearing of the site for construction. *John Uckley.*

Fort Payne, Alabama

The Fort Payne station is located fifty-one miles south of Chattanooga and ninety-three miles north of Birmingham in DeKalb County, Alabama. The station was originally built for the Alabama Great Southern Railroad Company, now the Southern Railway Company. The stone station was built in 1890/1891, the architect being Charles C. Taylor of Cincinnati, Ohio. Credit has also been given for its design to Mr. G. B. Nicholson, Chief Engineer of the Alabama Great Southern and the New Orleans & Texas Pacific Railway. It is believed that Mr. Nicholson assisted in some manner with the station's design by following the drawings made by the architect, as it was not uncommon for railroad's Chief Engineers' to supervise and even design many station buildings.

In 1888 Fort Payne was a very small town with less than 600 inhabitants. The next year saw the formation of the Fort Payne Iron and Coal Company, bringing investors and their money to the area. By 1890, when construction of the Fort Payne station started, the town's population had grown by more than four times its previous count. This great increase in population and the resulting trade and commerce required the railroad to erect separate freight and passenger station facilities so as to better handle the increase in business. In September 1890 the railroad purchased land from the iron and coal company for the erection of the passenger station that was to be one of the finest late-nineteenth-century railroad stations in Alabama. When the building was completed in 1891, the first train arrived there on October 21. Business continued through the height of the boom, which ended when the coal and iron ran out. The town's population eventually decreased to slightly over 1,000, but the station continued in service over the years until its service was discontinued in 1970.

The station is a one-and-one-half-story building that originally had a passenger-shelter annex. The structure is basically rectangular in

FORT PAYNE, ALABAMA. The Fort Payne station showing the corner tower at trackside. This station is one of the very few remaining buildings from the Fort Payne boom-town days of 1890. *Frank E. Ardrey, Jr.*

FORT PAYNE, ALABAMA. Looking down the line at Fort Payne station in this more recent view of August 1972. The stone-constructed building was erected between 1890 and 1891 for the Alabama Great Southern Railroad, now Southern Railway Company. *C. L. Andrews Photo, collection of Herbert H. Harwood, Jr.*

FORT PAYNE, ALABAMA. An April 1973 view of Fort Payne station from the baggage-end portion of the building. Note the addition of the end double door and the raised freight platform fronting it. *C. K. Marsh Photo, collection of Herbert H. Harwood, Jr.*

plan with a round, two-story tower. Exterior walls are of 18-inch-thick, gray-colored sandstone, with red-colored, cut-and-dressed sandstone used in all the trimmings, such as belt courses, sills, arches, lintels, etc. The roof of the main building is covered with black Virginia slate, with plate tin in the tower and galvanized iron used in the ridging and finials. The overall dimensions of the original building, including the covered end porch annex and veranda, were approximately 36 by 112 feet, which also gives allowances in the width for the projection of the corner tower.

Interior rooms originally contained a separate, large, women's waiting room that included the first floor tower area, its own fireplace, adjoining toilet room, and two separate entry doors on opposite side walls. The central section containing the two gables, at right angles to the long axis of the building, contained a ticket office, small storeroom, and stairs that gave access to the second-floor rooms. An equally large, men's waiting room, in likeness to the women's waiting room, also had its own fireplace, adjoining toilet room, and two separate entry doors opposite one another. Adjoining the men's room, and separated by a wall, is the large baggage-and-express room whose roof is lower than that of the principal passenger-facility portion of the building. On the rear side of the building at streetside, were a seven-foot-wide veranda that both waiting-room doors on that side opened to, and a porte cochere. A large, open, roof-covered porch was also on the baggage-room end of the building. This has since disappeared, and a large freight door has been installed at one corner of the end wall adjoining a freight platform. This door is not arched, as are the other large, freight doors on the sides.

The ticket office had separate ticket windows, one facing the men's waiting room and the other facing the women's waiting room. Part of one of the waiting rooms was altered to become a part of the office in 1954 when consolidation of passenger and freight was made. The station is not a large structure, but its grey cut stonework and general design give the impression of massiveness, with qualities and character of a baronial estate residence, which it could be taken for if it were not for the tracks and other station facilities surrounding it.

The Fort Payne station was chosen in 1966 for an Alabama Mountain Lake Association brochure, as a unique representation of Fort Payne. The Fort Payne Opera Building, another building remaining from the days of the boom-town era, is a companion structure to the station. The station still appears in good condition and exists today as a fine example of late-nineteenth-century, stone, railroad-station architecture in northern Alabama. It was placed on the National Register of Historic Places, with verification dated 1971.

Hamlet, North Carolina

Hamlet station in Richmond County, North Carolina, was built by the Seaboard Air Line Railroad in 1900 on property purchased in February of that year. Mr. Frank Shortridge, from whom the station property was purchased, gave much of the right-of-way property for this railroad and others whose lines passed through the town. The same year the station was built was also the time that the Seaboard Air Line Railroad Company was established from more than 180 railroad companies. The station was a principal link between the North and the South and was the main station of the railroad at that time. The station building contained offices for the railroad's North Carolina Division until 1944, when this unit was incorporated within other divisions. The offices of the North Carolina Division were, in addition to passenger-station facilities, contained in the building.

The original two-story, frame station had two wings, each facing tracks that cross, basically forming an L-shaped building with an imposing semicircular pavilion that projects out at the intersection of the two wings and faces the crossing junction of the tracks. The north wing is slightly longer and wider than the west wing, but both are of similar design and covered with a spreading gabled roof that joins the splayed, conical roof of the central pavilion. A series of triangular braces supports the continuous, roof overhang that extends a considerable distance on the upper main roof. The first-floor level also has an overhang roof that is even wider and that skirts the building in the same general manner as the main roof and acts as a shelter-cover over the surrounding trackside platform. A series of longer and stronger, angled brackets support this roof, which follows along the line of the upper main roof, giving a harmonious appearance to the entire building.

Doors and windows, in many cases, are irregularly spaced, differing from the original design due to remodeling. Windows on both levels are of the same large, one-over-one, rectangular sash, including those of the pavilion. The gabled ends of both wings have a narrowed-arched window, with two shorter windows flanking it. The west wing has a single-story frame addition extending from it.

During 1944, the station was expanded to include a two-story, brick addition placed perpendicularly to the end of the north wing, thus giving the building as a whole a U-shaped appearance that exists today. Remodeling was done to the original steps to the second floor in the following years.

The station was an important link in serving the armed-forces personnel during World War II. Though the interior of the wings has been altered considerably in arrangement, the main waiting room occupying the round pavilion

HAMLET, NORTH CAROLINA. The Hamlet station as it looked prior to its 1944 remodeling. Note the double set of crossing tracks in this view. It was basically an L-shaped building until a two-story addition was made in 1944. *Courtesy Seaboard Coast Line.*

HAMLET, NORTH CAROLINA. The Hamlet station as it looked on November 16, 1974, showing a bright new paint scheme. The sign at center, next to the second-floor windows, reads: Amtrak Rail Passenger Station. *R. D. Patton Photo.*

HAMLET, NORTH CAROLINA. Hamlet station, showing one wing of the building as it looked on June 16, 1976. Note the air conditioners in some of the second floor windows. *Howard W. Ameling.*

HAMLET, NORTH CAROLINA. A June 1976 view showing one end wing with attached single-story structures. Note the brick chimney projecting through the roof overhang at the end of the original main building. *Howard W. Ameling.*

HAMLET, NORTH CAROLINA. A June 1976 view showing the direct-end portion of one wing, the brick-addition wing, platform shelter at left along one of the main lines, and a branch line that curves past the rear area of the station at right. *Howard W. Ameling.*

HAMLET, NORTH CAROLINA. The rear-portion view of Hamlet station, showing additions to the original building as it looked in June 1976. *Howard W. Ameling.*

remains as originally designed, including the ticket office in the inner portion of the angle. The second floor of the pavilion still retains the dispatching office.

In July 1967, the Seaboard Air Line Railroad was merged to become a part of the Seaboard Coast Line Railroad that now owns the Hamlet station. The station has been repainted in fresh, bright colors and, since World War II, has served mainly as a stop for the resorts in the region. At the time of this writing, the Hamlet station still serves as a rail passenger station, though the railroad is considering a replacement for it with a more modern station facility near the old station. Local town officials have made plans to retain the existing Hamlet station for use as a railroad museum. This seems an appropriate choice, related to the growth and development of the town that resulted from the coming of the railroad to Hamlet.

The Hamlet station remains today in excellent condition with very few alterations. It was placed on the National Register of Historic Places, with verification dated 1971.

Howell, Michigan

The Howell depot is located in Livingston County, Michigan, and was built in the summer of 1886 by the Toledo, Ann Arbor, and Northern Michigan Railway Company, which in 1895 became the Ann Arbor Railroad Company. Promoters for the TAA&NM were circulating in the early part of 1885 to choose new routes through Livingston and Shiawassee Counties. The Detroit, Lansing and Northern Railroad Company was already serving Howell, whose residents wanted the TAA&NM line also, so as to provide competitive shipping rates and greatly benefit the town. Howell residents voted to raise funds of $20,000 to induce the railroad to enter Howell, as several other towns were also competing for inclusion on the new line, but Howell succeeded in obtaining the route.

As the new line proceeded, hostility erupted between the two rival railroads in January 1886, regarding which railroad would build a bridge where the two lines crossed along the right of way. Gangs of armed workmen from the two railroads clashed, and former Ohio Congressman James Ashley, also president of the TAA&NM, was arrested in the brawl. The case was finally settled in court in favor of the TAA&NM, and, after a year-and-a-half of struggle to bring the line north from Ann Arbor through Livingston County, curving through and terminating at Frankfort on Lake Michigan, the line was completed in the fall of 1886. The new Howell depot had been erected earlier that summer.

The depot is positioned on a site two blocks from the center of town at the end of Walnut Street. The rectangular shaped building, approximately 22 by 50 feet, is of brick construction with a bay window. A single, centrally located, brick chimney tops the gabled roof now covered with modern, rolled roofing. The roof overhang is supported by a series of matching, curved, ornate braces on both sides and ends, which are an attractive feature of the depot's architecture. The tops of all windows are shallow arched with sliding sash. Decorative, curved, cast hoods surmount doors and windows, and doors have paned lights over them, giving added light, on a level with the top arches of the windows, so as to harmonize on an even level in their series. The gabled ends have small circular openings with a star pattern over which is a semicircular, cast hood. The corners of the building brickwork stand out slightly giving an inbuilt column effect. Stepped brick patterns are also found in the gabled ends adjoining the inner roof line and within the columned, corner projections.

There are presently three rooms in the depot with 18-foot-high ceilings, 4-foot-high wainscoting, and planked 2-foot-wide floorboards. The Ann Arbor Railroad ceased running passenger trains to Howell in June 1950, with freight

HOWELL, MICHIGAN. The Howell, Michigan station was built in 1886 and serves today as the Livingston County Historical Society's Depot Museum. The station has been restored to its present excellent condition, as seen in this 1974 view. *John Uckley.*

HOWELL, MICHIGAN. A four-wheeled inspection car in front of the Howell station in 1914, with the station agent, John D. Hamilton, standing at extreme right. The other persons are unidentified. Note in the background the single-stall engine house which no longer exists. *Courtesy Chester F. Clark, Livingston County Historical Society.*

HOWELL, MICHIGAN. A 1914 interior view of the Howell station, with station agent John D. Hamilton seated and Will Wright standing. The calendar on the wall is of January 1914, but the flier on the desk says: "Go to church Sunday, Mar. 22." The station agent later became the first director of the Detroit Edison Electric office in Howell. *Courtesy Chester F. Clark, Livingston County Historical Society.*

HOWELL, MICHIGAN. A June 1974 view of the Howell station, showing the building's location with respect to the tracks and other buildings in the immediate area. *John Uckley.*

HOWELL, MICHIGAN. The roof overhang is supported by a series of matching, curved, ornate braces that are an attractive feature of the station's architecture as seen in this trackside view of June 1974. *John Uckley.*

HOWELL, MICHIGAN. A new, chain-link fence was placed along the tracks and at one end of the property as a safety measure, since trains still use the line in the foreground. *John Uckley.*

HOWELL, MICHIGAN. The restored Howell station as it looked November 5, 1975, showing the street side at right and tracks at left. *John Uckley.*

service continuing. In 1970, the Livingston County Historical Society purchased the depot and operates it as a depot museum. Not long after the depot was acquired by the society, it was painted red, with cream-color trimmings. Landscaping around the depot was also improved. Much of this improvement was done in the summer of 1970 when the Howell high school offered a course in museum techniques, and the class assisted in its restoration.

The railroad still leases an east-end section of the depot for shipping activities, but the single-track Ann Arbor main line between Toledo, Ohio and Frankfort, Michigan has very little traffic. Such traffic consists mainly of Penn Central coal trains and one Ann Arbor freight train each way rumbling daily past the depot. The Ann Arbor's leased space in the depot is expected to expire soon, leaving that space to the Livingston County Historical Society for its continued use as a depot museum.

The Howell depot is an important structure symbolizing the growth of the town and is a reminder of earlier times when the town had seen bitter rivalry between the railroads. A plaque mounted on a stand outside the depot tells briefly of this conflict and notes that the property is a Michigan Historical Commission Registered local site. The Howell depot was also placed on the National Register of Historic Places, with verification dated 1971.

HOWELL, MICHIGAN. A plaque mounted outside the station gives a brief account of the dispute and notes that the property is a Michigan Historical Commission Registered local site. *John Uckley.*

Ida, Michigan

The first Lake Shore and Michigan Southern office in Ida was located in the Rauch Hotel and Wayside Inn, which was in operation at the time of the coming of the railroad in 1840. The original railroad, the Southern Michigan Railroad, followed an earlier southern route at the city of Monroe, Michigan, using a horse drawn line that had already been established there, and ran between LaPlaisance Bay, on Lake Erie, and Monroe, Michigan. The route, laid out to go westward to terminate at Buffalo on Lake Michigan, was completed as far as Hillside in 1846 when financial problems with the Southern Michigan Railroad finally halted construction of rail in all directions, resulting in the railroad's being sold that same year. By the time of the Civil War, many smaller lines consolidated to form the Lake Shore and Michigan Southern Railroad. The line between Monroe and Adrian in Michigan was completed and continued in service until, in 1914, the L.S. & M.S. became part of the New York Central System formed from the merger of the New York Central and Hudson River Railroad. These lines became part of the Penn Central merger in 1967.

In 1875, a new depot was built at Ida on the Lake Shore and Michigan Southern line between Monroe and Adrian, Michigan. This was the original Ida depot that was built by the railroad when it was felt that a separate structure was needed to serve the traveling public and the local freight and shipping companies. This depot was a rectangular wood frame building, with office and passenger area at one end and freight room at the opposite end. A siding track ran along one side of the depot, close to a wood-planked, elevated platform used mainly for freight handling from the cars to and from the freight room. The windows were rectangular in shape in the passenger portion, with large, freight doors only on the freight portion of the building. Exterior walls were of vertical boards, with small trimming pieces set in at all the joint intervals around the structure. A wide, wooded stairway gave access to both the loading platform and the depot's front-end main entrance. Rainwater gutters ran along both sides of the sloping roof to downspouts. There was a single, brick chimney located about midway between the passenger- and freight-room areas that was connected to a potbelly stove within the passenger-office area that can be seen through the open door in one of the photographs. The single-story structure's floor was elevated to a level even with the outside freight platform.

The depot at Ida continued in service until the evening of February 23, 1923, when a fire, which completely destroyed the building, broke out at 7:45 P.M. Louie Englehart, the depot agent, was first on the scene, but it was

IDA, MICHIGAN. The original Ida depot of the Lake Shore and Michigan Southern, located on a branch line that ran between Monroe and westward to Adrian, Michigan. It's summer 1890 as the agent poses in front of the office and passenger end of the depot. The small sign between the door and window reads: "American Express Co. Agency." Note the horizontal, wood, telegraph-wire support at left, just above the hanging lantern. *John Uckley Collection.*

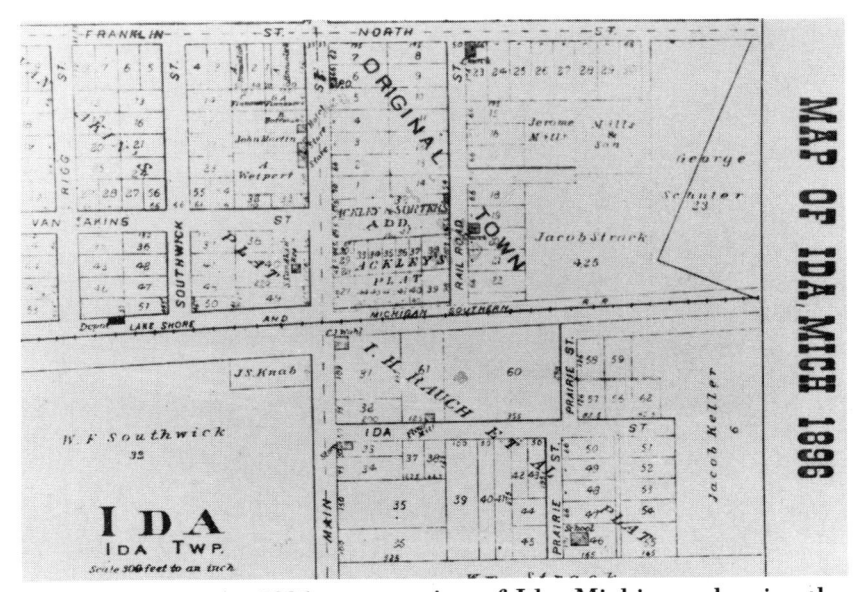

IDA, MICHIGAN. An 1896 map portion of Ida, Michigan, showing the Lake Shore and Michigan Southern line passing the Ida depot at left center. *Cavalier Collection.*

IDA, MICHIGAN. Ida depot in the Fall of 1890, showing the freight platform and tracks. The potbellied stove can been seen through the open door. A new sign has been added, upper left of the door frame, reading: "Western Union Telegraph & Cable Office." The horizontal, wood, telegraph-wire support, seen in the 1890 summer view, has been removed, and a new telegraph pole installed directly in front of the end door near the foot of the steps. Note the short, wood, canopy pieces over the doors and windows. *John Uckley Collection.*

IDA, MICHIGAN. Lake Shore and Michigan Southern locomotive No. 242 stops for a pose with crew. The photo is undated, but the locomotive is typical of steam power used after the American Civil War hauling passengers and freight from Erie, Pennsylvania, to Chicago, Illinois, passing Ida daily. *Collection of Everett J. Payette.*

IDA, MICHIGAN. A Lake Shore and Michigan Southern early steam locomotive, hauling a short passenger train, on the tracks that ran on one side and off the cobblestone road in Ida. *Collection of Everett J. Payette.*

IDA, MICHIGAN. On its way to Ida, Michigan, this train is leaving Front Street in Monroe, Michigan, as seen in this view of June 9, 1917. Such trains were used daily by commuters to and from the city and were typical of those along the line during this period. *Collection of Everett J. Payette.*

IDA, MICHIGAN. It is the evening of February 23, 1923. A fire in the Ida depot started at 7:45 P.M. Louie Englehart, the agent at this time, was the first person on the scene. A bucket brigade was formed in an attempt to control the blaze, but nothing could stop the spreading flames that reduced the building to a skeleton frame. Many valuable papers and much freight were lost. A photographer on the scene recorded the disaster. *John Uckley Collection.*

IDA, MICHIGAN. The smoldering ruins of the Ida depot. When the westbound passenger train arrived the next morning, this is what greeted it, to the astonishment of passengers and crew. A pullman car was moved near the site and used as a temporary depot until a new building could be built. *John Uckley Collection.*

IDA, MICHIGAN. The new Ida depot as it looked years after it was built in 1924. This view of 1952 shows branch-line activity with a New York Central train passing the depot. The Lake Shore and Michigan Southern was eventually acquired by the New York Central. Steam-powered locomotives continued in operation here until 1953 when they were discontinued, a year after this view was taken. *John Uckley Collection.*

IDA, MICHIGAN. The second Ida depot as it looked in 1968. The depot was abandoned in 1955. Note the elevated, freight platform at left, next to the depot whose windows had been boarded up years before. Part of the Monroe to Adrian line was severed in 1953 between Ida and Monroe. This depot was eventually demolished in the early 1970s. *Collection of Everett J. Payette.*

too late to save the depot, even though a bucket brigade had been quickly formed. Many valuable papers and much freight of the railroad were lost in the flames that quickly spread, burning the entire structure to the ground, save for a portion of the platform and steps and a few remaining studs that eventually fell into the rubble that remained. Fortunately no strong wind was blowing that might have otherwise fanned the blaze to other nearby dwellings, perhaps destroying the entire village. As the train arrived the next morning only the charred remains greeted the astonished passengers.

Since Ida was an important stop along the line, plans were immediately put into effect to erect a new depot. In the meantime, while construction of the new facility was under way, a Pullman car was moved into position and used as a temporary depot. The new Ida depot, located on the site of the original Ida depot, was started in 1923 and completed in 1924. This new depot continued in service until 1955 when it was abandoned after express service was discontinued, though freight service to grain and beet farmers of the area continued. The second Ida depot was boarded up, as seen In the 1968 photograph, and eventually was demolished in the early 1970s. Passenger service had ended in the 1930-31 period. Eventually the tracks were removed to the east edge of the village to continue rail service to grain elevators, but the heavily laden cars could no longer operate on the rails, and the service was later replaced with large semitrailer trucks.

An old handbill was located for the year 1908 that indicated, in part, the following:

This handbill announces an excursion trip to Detroit on the Lake Shore and Michigan Southern Railroad. Excursion to Detroit, Saturday April 18 and 25, 1908, over the Lake Shore and Michigan Southern Railroad.

The trains passed through Ida at 9:34 A.M. and the fare to Detroit from Ida was 75 cents.

The original depot at Ida will be long remembered by the local residents as its first center of transportation and commerce, as days of excursions and reunions, and as a long-gone center of attractions as the trains arrived and departed on daily schedules, carrying passengers and freight to and from the community. The trains' dependability had provided the largest means of transportation for the entire area along the line, and the Ida depot, once the center of activity, is now only a faded memory of what life in that community once was.

Ladson, South Carolina

Ladson station is the smallest railroad structure presented in this work and was selected for its uniqueness and for the special character it displays in its architecture. It was also selected to illustrate the ornate qualities of its design that is most attractive to the eye, yet serving as a functioning station facility suitable for the little community it served at the time.

The Ladson station was built in the 1880s by the South Carolina Railway, a predecessor of the Southern Railway. It was originally constructed in the village of Summerville in Dorchester County, South Carolina, where it served for a short time. It was later moved on flat cars to Ladson in north Charleston County, South Carolina, about eight miles southeast of Summerville. Ladson was a small community located only about fifteen miles northwest of the city of Charleston, S.C.

The station basically consisted of two small, separate but related structures placed side by side on the site next to the tracks and fronting a long ground-level platform area. The larger, major building served mainly as a telegraph and ticket office, and the minor smaller building adjacent to it was used mainly as a freight shed but also as an open shelter for passengers; both buildings were of wood-frame construction.

The principal building was a single-room, rectangular structure, basically of board and batten construction, and having an unusually high ceiling for its size. The entry at trackside is centrally located and has two narrow doors that opened inward, with a smaller window above it within the door framing. The windows were one-over-one sash, each with six lights, all having the same design on all walls of the building. All windows had sloping cresting, and the two windows facing the freight shed had extra-ornate, carved, Gothic-styled hoods, not found on any of the other windows. It is believed that, when the station was first built at the Summerville site, all its windows had these ornate, Gothic-style hoods.

The graceful curvature of the gabled roof and its decorative bracket supports are perhaps the outstanding features of this little building. The roof was of asphalt shingles, but heavily tarred over for waterproofing, which gives it its smooth appearance. Both gabled ends are of identical style and design, with the carved, roof-overhang brackets on the sides only. A large, circular, carved, crest design is also found centered on both end walls within the gables. Carved center poles project through the roof peak at both ends, extending above and below, adding to the elaborate ornamentation of the overall design. It is believed that a sheet-metal chimney stack once projected through the peak at center of the roof but was later removed when the station was relocated. This may have

LADSON, SOUTH CAROLINA. Ladson station was built in the 1880s by the South Carolina Railway. The small, ornate structure was originally located at Summerville, S.C., but moved on flat cars to Ladson, about eight miles from Summerville. The station continued in service until 1935 when it was dismantled. *Courtesy Southern Railway.*

LADSON, SOUTH CAROLINA. This is a later view of Ladson, showing the train-order post moved to another position off the building. The ornamentation on the structure illustrates a time when such attention to detail was a consideration for the elegance and importance of the structure to the community. *Courtesy Southern Railway.*

LADSON, SOUTH CAROLINA. A partial view, showing detail of the gabled-end trimmings and windows. Note the position of the trian-order board passing through the roof overhang. *Southern Railway, Cavalier Collection.*

LADSON, SOUTH CAROLINA. In this later view, the train-order board has been relocated, mounted to a ground pole, and passes the outside roof eave. *Southern Railway, Cavalier Collection.*

LADSON, SOUTH CAROLINA. The small, freight shed, detached from the main building, is less elaborate in its trimmings. Note the portion of a small, flat, section car, in the open part of the shed, that was housed there. A portion of an open, raised platform is seen at extreme right, next to the shed. *Southern Railway, Cavalier Collection.*

led to a potbellied stove within, and some roof patching at the stack's probable location, that does not match the rest of the roofing, seems to confirm this belief. In comparing the two station photographs presented here, taken at different periods, the train-order-board post is located through the lower part of the roof overhang in the earlier view. The later view shows it was relocated, adjoining the edge of the roof overhang and extended and braced at ground level. The exterior walls of both buildings had a two-tone paint scheme, with white on the trimmings and carved ornamentation.

The smaller, freight building has an enclosed and adjoining open section, both covered by a single-gabled-shingled roof, with ridging along its peak. A small, brick chimney at the enclosed end of the structure gives evidence of some form of heating provision for it. The roof overhang extends out further at trackside for added shelter and is supported simply by wood braces at the ends, with square, slender, wood posts on both sides, also having braces flaring from them. The gabled ends have board and batten siding, with angled, wood siding below on the enclosed portion and on the wall at the end of the open shed. At the far end of the open shed portion was a wide, raised platform of timber construction that had a planked floor. The platform floor was on an elevation with freight car floors, so freight could be transferred directly and easily on an even level.

The Ladson station existed in service for about fifty years. In 1935 it was dismantled, thus ending a unique style of small flag-stop, combination-type railroad station design of a bygone era. Though Ladson station was a small, quaint structure, it was a functioning facility that displayed a character of its own from an earlier time when thoughtful design and workmanship were important considerations of the railroads. The ornate trimmings were also an important part of earlier wood-frame building designs used extensively at that time. Thus, Ladson station had the pleasing quality of appearance to which people of the period were generally accustomed. Such designs added some measure of status to the small community at a time when pleasant surroundings and quality craftsmanship were major considerations for passengers.

Lebanon, Pennsylvania

The Lebanon station was built in 1885 and designed by George W. Hewitt, a noted architect who was in partnership with his brother William and had designed many other outstanding buildings in Philadelphia. The Cornwall & Lebanon Railroad station at Lebanon, in Lebanon County, Pennsylvania, was built for Robert Colman, the iron-ore millionaire of that time. The C & L was a short line railroad, with only twenty-two miles of track from Conewago, east of Harrisburg on the Pennsylvania Railroad's main line. It was probably the great wealth of Robert Colman that allowed for the architectural quality of the grand station building for such a small railroad.

Architecturally, the station is a blend of late-nineteenth-century Victorian style in combination with Romanesque and Flemish styles. When the station was originally built in 1885, it was rectangular in design, with one wing off to one side. In 1912, the south wing was extended and other major alterations were made. The wing extension allowed for inclusion of offices for a railway express company, and the architectural style was retained in keeping with the original structure, so that today it is difficult to determine that an addition had been made. During the 1912 addition, the entire interior of the building was remodeled, and at the present time much of the interior wainscoting, mouldings, fireplaces, and other interior fittings still remain.

The building is two stories, with attic space, and is basically of brick construction, with a cut-stone base that extends just above the first-floor window sills. The structure features highly decorative, stepped gables, arched and shallow-arched windows found mainly on the second floor. A Chateauesque influence is also evident in the gabled, hipped roof, and some trimmings and window styles. Terra-cotta is used extensively, and such ornamented designs and trimmings are evident on the upper portions of all exterior walls. The roof peaks still have some of the decorative, patterned cresting, and much other ornamentation is still intact on the roof. Wide, porch shelters still remain, with their original, intricately designed iron brackets. At one time an iron-frame shed was located along the north wall and used originally as a shelter for trains waiting to depart. This shelter no longer exists today, having been demolished many years ago.

Lebanon was an active station facility during the time the Cornwall & Lebanon Railroad was in service. The line, which ran from Lebanon to Conewago, Pennsylvania, on the Pennsylvania Railroad main line, was purchased by the Pennsylvania Railroad in 1918. Passenger service ended in the 1930s. It was a Pennsylvania Railroad branch during most of its existence and, since 1968, is a part of Penn Central. A part

LEBANON, PENNSYLVANIA. The Cornwall and Lebanon Railroad station in an early view taken after the passenger train shed, seen at right, was built, but which no longer exists. The station was large and very elaborate for a short-line railroad, but active and a major center for the town. *Cavalier Collection.*

LEBANON, PENNSYLVANIA. The Lebanon station building as it looked in September 1975, existing in its new role as the Robel Frocks, Inc. The former station building has been restored considerably and is now well maintained. The passenger train shed had long since been removed. *David P. Oroszi.*

LEBANON, PENNSYLVANIA. A street and trackside angled view. The station was built in 1885, with major additions made in 1912. Passenger service ended in the 1930s. *David P. Oroszi.*

LEBANON, PENNSYLVANIA. A trackside view taken in September 1975. Though the large, passenger-train shed no longer exists, the smaller, attached shelter remains, with its ornamented iron braces intact. *David P. Oroszi.*

LEBANON, PENNSYLVANIA. Corner view of the building with fire escape addition. Note the ornamented shelter braces and architectural detail of the upper, arched windows and trimmings. *David P. Oroszi.*

LEBANON, PENNSYLVANIA. Terra-cotta is used extensively in the ornamented designs and trimmings on all exterior upper-wall portions. Some fragments of the original roof cresting are still visible. *David P. Oroszi.*

LEBANON, PENNSYLVANIA. Extensively intricate designs are still clearly visible on the upper-story windows and frieze as well as on the series of iron-shed roof braces, as seen in this view of September 1975. *David P. Oroszi.*

LEBANON, PENNSYLVANIA. A close-up view of a portion of the upper, exterior wall and roof portion, showing decorative design trimmings that are extensive throughout the upper-exterior walls and chimneys. *David P. Oroszi.*

LEBANON, PENNSYLVANIA. An end-wall facade close-up view showing the design detail and stepped brickwork that is still well preserved and intact. *David P. Oroszi.*

of the line was washed out during the Hurricane Agnes flood of June 1972, and, since then, it has been largely out of service. What remains of the property is part of Conrail.

The Lebanon station building has been improved considerably in the past few years from its previous unmaintained condition. Architecturally, it is a very fine example of late-nineteenth-century railroad-station architecture that still displays much of its intricately detailed ornamentation and patterned designs. The station building was placed on the National Register of Historic Places, with verification dated 1974. The building exists today and is used by the Robel Frocks, Incorporated. It is now well-preserved, even though some alterations and additions have been made to facilitate the use of the building by the firm. These alterations have not destroyed the many fine architectural features of the building, and its appearance is much the same today as it was when in active service many years ago.

Liberty, Indiana

The Liberty depot was built in 1902, originally for passenger service only with baggage handling facilities, and was the second depot on this site. It is located seventy-one miles east of Indianapolis in Union County, on the Baltimore and Ohio Railroad's Indianapolis, Indiana, to Hamilton, Ohio, main line. The depot was originally on the line of the Cincinnati, Indianapolis, and Western Railroad, later the Cincinnati, Hamilton and Dayton Railway on their Indianapolis Division, eventually to become part of the Baltimore and Ohio Railroad.

This interesting brick-and-wood-frame depot originally contained a centrally located office, with a two-story bay at trackside. Separate ladies' and men's waiting rooms flanked the office area, and each of these waiting rooms had its own toilet room. The two waiting rooms and office were connected by a short hallway. A small, baggage room is located at one corner of the building with its own separate, exterior, large, sliding, freight door at the end of the building. Three brick chimneys are centrally located on the roof peak at approximately equal intervals and originate from the office and both waiting rooms. A small, coal room in one corner of the men's room indicated coal stoves were originally used for the heating system of the building.

The depot is basically a rectangular-shaped structure about 90 by 24 feet and was surrounded by a ground-level, brick platform close to the exterior walls and extending out from either end of the building along trackside. The exterior walls below the window sills are brick, with horizontal siding from the bottom sills up to the top of the walls, terminating at the roof line. An interesting architectural feature of the design is the angled, roof-overhang braces. These are all solid, encased with the same siding material used on the upper, exterior-wall portions. The roof overhangs these braces slightly, extending outward almost in line with the bay window, and accents the roof overhang around the entire building. Another most attractive feature is the older-style, large, arched, multipaned, glass windows that combine well with the smooth lines of the siding.

Some revisions have been made to the building over the years. With the eventual passing of passenger service at Liberty, the depot was converted for freight-only service. At the rear wall of the former, ladies' waiting room, a large, freight door was installed where one of the triwindow sections once was. This room thus became a freight room for truck loading and unloading as the small baggage room was too tiny for this purpose. The trackside window of this same room was also revised for installation of another large, freight door. A small, raised, wood-planked platform with steps was built on the exterior, adjoining this new door, and is still

LIBERTY, INDIANA. A 1908 view of the Liberty, Indiana, station, just six years after it was built, showing the original design. The second-story bay and all chimney caps were later removed, as were the fenced lawns at both ends of the station. Note the other buildings behind the station at right; these would also change with the passing of time. *Mark J. Camp Collection.*

LIBERTY, INDIANA. The Liberty depot as it looked on April 1, 1954—a view facing the baggage end of the building. Note that the chimney caps had been removed, but the second-story, bay portion is still intact. The train-order board is also in its original position. *Max Miller.*

LIBERTY, INDIANA. Liberty depot as it looked on August 24, 1963. The building is basically the same in design although several alterations had been made, such as the removal of the second-story, bay portion and the relocation of the train-order-board signal. Note the platform along trackside is still intact. *Max Miller Photo, C. L. Andrews Collection.*

LIBERTY, INDIANA. The Liberty depot on August 25, 1974, when the building was no longer in service but prior to the boarding up of the windows and doors. Note that the curb of the platform along trackside has been removed. Comparison of this view with the 1908 view shows considerble changes to the building and buildings at the rear of the depot at right. *David P. Oroszi.*

LIBERTY, INDIANA. Liberty depot on March 9, 1975, showing all windows and doors boarded up. The train-order-board signal had been removed earlier. *David P. Oroszi.*

LIBERTY, INDIANA. A March 1975 view showing the rear-street side portion of the depot. Note that the roof overhang along the rear side is shorter than it is on both ends and along trackside. *David P. Oroszi.*

LIBERTY, INDIANA. Looking toward the baggage-room end of the depot at trackside on March 9, 1975. A comparison can be made with the 1954 view. *David P. Oroszi.*

there today. The ground-level, brick, platform walk was removed, or covered over with gravel, to allow for freight service activities and truck movements in the rear area. The floor of the former, ladies' waiting room, at the locations of the two freight doors, was elevated on a level with the base of these doors to allow for the easy handling of freight on a common level.

Sometime between 1954 and 1963, the second-story portion of the bay at trackside was removed. The original, wide, chimney caps of brick, seen in the 1908 photo view presentd here, had been removed several years before the second-story bay was removed. These two exterior revisions gave the depot an overall effect of being a more modernly designed building in appearance, with a hint of old-style quality.

The recent color of the depot roof is a bright red; the wood siding, including the small, brick portion around the lower part of the bay window, is yellow. The three chimneys are their natural-red-brick color, and the brickwork around the base of the windows below the sills was originally the natural-red-brick color, but had eventually been painted over at one time with a dull, red paint.

The Liberty depot continued in active service until 1972 when it was closed. The last agent was Raymond R. Ross. All the windows were boarded up and the building abandoned after seventy years of service. Liberty depot still exists at this writing and is structurally sound; but its future is uncertain.

Lincoln, Nebraska

The Chicago, Rock Island and Pacific Railroad Company completed a railroad line through Lincoln, in Lancaster County, Nebraska, in 1893. Construction of a railroad station in the Chateauesque style of architecture was begun in October 1892. Mr. Eugene Woerner of Lincoln served as general contractor during construction, using plans for the building prepared under the direction of Chief Engineer, R. W. Day, of the Rock Island line.

Original floor plans, made during some revisions of January 1919, show the main building of the station as having a centrally located general waiting room, a bay-windowed ticket office, a semicircular, smoking room at one corner, with adjoining toilet room, and directly opposite on the same side, a semicircular, ladies' room, also with adjoining toilet room.

At one end of the main building is an open, waiting platform and, at the direct opposite end, a detached, baggage room and adjoining boiler room. The roof of the main building extends out on different levels to both of these areas, so as to give an overall effect of continuous roofing, but with different designs and levels projecting from low-bracketed eaves of the respective building sections.

When construction was completed, the grand opening of the red-sandstone and brick station occurred on May 7, 1893. It was considered one of Nebraska's finest examples of nineteenth-century railroad architecture. The station continued in service for more than seventy years, until the Rock Island Railroad discontinued its passenger service through Lincoln in 1966.

The City National Bank of Lincoln was looking for a branch bank building in the late 1960s. Nebraska law stated that such a branch had to be within a half mile of the main bank office building. The bank's president, Ronald H. Tornblom, had to make a search for a suitable building that would both fill the needs of the bank and be within the required distance of the main bank office. The old Lincoln station had been vacant and in need of repairs for some time, and the railroad was soon to abandon it. The station, which is located alongside the tracks, was selected as an ideal building that filled the necessary requirements. Although the railroad continued to use its trackage next to the station for freight transport, the building was still structurally sound and reusable. The original, exterior walls had been painted over, the roof needed replacement, and several other deteriorating parts of the building would need to be repaired. In 1968, the City National Bank purchased the station building from the Rock Island Railroad to be used as their new branch bank.

In the year that followed, the bank, in addition to its initial purchase price for the

LINCOLN, NEBRASKA. The Lincoln, Nebraska, station, as it looked on June 15, 1920. The station was originally built in 1892 by the Chicago, Rock Island and Pacific Railroad and served as a passenger station until 1966. *Nebraska State Historical Society, Lincoln, Nebraska.*

LINCOLN, NEBRASKA. Lincoln station on April 8, 1968. The railroad had painted the brickwork, as shown in this view. The paint was removed when the building was restored several years later. *William F. Rapp, Jr.*

LINCOLN, NEBRASKA. A trackside view, showing the baggage-room end of the building taken when the station was still in active railroad service. *Nebraska State Historical Society, Lincoln, Nebraska.*

LINCOLN, NEBRASKA. A more recent view of the former Lincoln station, showing it in its restored condition and with a new pedestrian-protection fence added along track-side. The tracks have also changed, as seen in comparison with other views presented here. *Nebraska State Historical Society, Lincoln, Nebraska.*

VICKSBURG, MISSISSIPPI. The Vicksburg station as it looked in the spring of 1962, at which time the building was still well-maintained. Built in 1906, the basic structure still remains much the same as when constructed. Although it has deteriorated in recent years, it still retains much of its original character. The building is still in use today, but there is some question regarding its future existence. *Robert W. O'Brien.*

WHITEHALL STATION, BRYN MAWR, PENNSYLVANIA. The lower street-level portion of the building is seen in this view of December 1975 of the former Pennsylvania Railroad's Whitehall station. Built in 1859, originally by the old Philadelphia & Columbia Railroad, the Whitehall station still exists and is in use today as a thrift shop. The building has outlasted its replacement station, a stone structure once located in Bryn Mawr. Whitehall station is a very fine example of wood-frame railroad-station architecture of pre-Civil War days of which only a very few survive. *Robert Storks.*

building, invested a considerable amount of money to restore and repair the station. During 1969, the bank obtained the services of architects to restore the building to its original style, with the very minimum number of modifications, while converting a portion of the interior to serve as a Depot Drive-Up banking facility.

The major alterations and repairs to the station building's exterior included sandblasting of the exterior walls to remove the old wall paint and placement of new roofing material on the entire multileveled roofs. The interior was remodeled only as necessary, so as to retain as much as possible of the original decor. Original railroad furnishings, secured from other old depots in Nebraska, were installed in the renovated station. Such items as a waiting-room bench from Burlington's depot at Wilbur and a potbelly stove from the Chicago and North Western's Exetor depot were among the items that added to the old-time atmosphere of the station. Other furnishings in the bank's new facility included rolltop desks, older-styled lounge chairs, and numerous other railroad artifacts that blend well with the decor and use of the station.

By the summer of 1969, work on the banking facility was completed, and on June 23 of that year the new branch bank, the "Citibank Depot Drive-Up," celebrated its grand opening. In 1970, an unused portion of the building was converted into rental space and eventually was occupied that year by a gift shop.

With the continued disappearance of railroad stations in North America, the efforts of the bank to restore such a structure to a useful purpose had proved a successful investment not only for the bank but for the community as well. Residents of Lincoln and visitors now have the pleasure of viewing an exceptionally fine example of Chateauesque-style architecture, as well as knowing its presence can continue to give a sense of stability, even on this small scale, in ever changing surroundings. At the same time, the building serves a useful and beneficial function for both its occupants and the public.

For its excellent restoration, the station has received a certificate of commendation from the American Association for State and Local History of Nashville, Tennessee, in addition to other local awards for a fine example of civic improvement in Lincoln. The station is also listed on the National Register of Historic Places, with verification dated 1971, as well as on the Nebraska Historical Society Register. The station exists today as an active, useful building that benefits both its owners and the community, while continuing as a very fine example of late-nineteenth-century railroad architecture.

Medford, Oregon

The existing Medford depot was built by the Southern Pacific Railroad in 1911 and is located thirty miles south of Grants Pass in southern Oregon on the Eugene, Oregon, to Redding, California main line. This depot replaced the first Southern Pacific depot that was located on Main and Front Streets within sight of Riddle House, once a hotel and restaurant. The proximity of both the old depot and the hotel resulted in intense activity in Medford both in passenger and freight traffic passing north and south along the line. Transport by stage coach and rail was established there, and the old Medford depot served in handling both passenger and freight traffic.

Passenger facilities at the old depot were very limited, as the one-and-one-half-story, wood-frame, rectangular building was a combination depot but mainly designed to handle freight. Tracks ran on both sides of the building, which had a raised platform at one

MEDFORD, OREGON. The first Southern Pacific depot at Medford, Oregon, on Main and Front Streets. This interesting view, taken in the mid-1880s, shows the depot at left and Riddle House at right, once a hotel and restaurant. A busy day at the depot long ago. *Southern Pacific.*

MEDFORD, OREGON. Stage coaches and wagons line up with visitors and town folk for a pose in this view taken in 1887. The Medford depot is directly at center in this rare photo. *Southern Pacific.*

MEDFORD, OREGON. A northeast-corner view of the old Medford depot taken about 1900. The wide, roof overhang is well illustrated here, with the bay window facing the main line tracks. This depot was replaced in 1911 by another wood-frame depot. *Southern Pacific.*

end, along one side, and continued in a sloping ramp at the other end, with a wood, hand railing at the ramp end only. The large, oversized, gabled roof dominated the structure with wide overhangs at both sides and ends supported by braces on all sides, so that it acted as a shelter. The gabled ends had decorative, triangular-shaped, carved fillings at the extreme ends of the roof, centered by a small, vertical post that extended above and below the filling design. A bay window was on the passenger side, with no raised platform along this frontage. All freight doors were elevated, and windows were rectangular in shape on both levels. The depot was covered with horizontal siding on the exterior walls above the lower-floor window sills, with vertical boards and battens on the bay-window side and the visible portion along the ramp end. The freight platform extended about the same distance as the roof overhang, with planked, platform top enclosed all around the sides by vertical boards.

The old Medford depot served the area for many years during the latter part of the nineteenth and early part of the twentieth centuries. But business had increased continually as the territory and the town of Medford developed and in 1911 a new and larger combination depot was built to handle the increased traffic in both passenger and freight service.

The new Southern Pacific Railroad's Medford depot is a long rectangular wood frame building, 34 by 165 feet, with passenger facilities at one end and a large, freight section at the other. The depot is basically a single-story structure with an attic-space room above and near the division of the passenger and freight sections. The main roof is hipped with a

MEDFORD, OREGON. The new Medford depot as it looked in 1911, seen in part behind the train in this slightly unfocused view. The area has built up considerably since this view was taken shortly after the depot was built. *Southern Pacific.*

MEDFORD, OREGON. The new Medford depot as it looked in April 1967. The depot still exists and is used now to house traffic and operations offices. The roof-cresting ridges have been removed, but the building is basically the same as it was when built. *Stan F. Styles.*

shorter, gabled roof at right angles to the long axis that covers the upper, attic room. The original roofing had ridging that was removed when new roofing was applied years later. The roof overhang is supported by a series of curved brackets, with shorter solid brackets supporting the slight overhang of the attic roof. The original, ornate, brick chimney still survives and is located on the passenger side of the building.

Horizontal siding covers the wood-frame much like a large dormer. Windows are rectangular, with movable lower sash. The windows on the lower floor have an additional light section, multipaned within the framing that encloses each window. The upper, attic section and section below it on the first floor project out from the building. The lower section was once a bay window but has since been altered, with the main side windows of the bay closed with siding. The wide, elevated, wood platform at trackside now extends to the end of the bay window, with steps terminating from it. The freight room also has an elevated floor on a level with the platform, so that freight can be easily handled from freight cars all at the same floor level.

As passenger service declined, the depot was used for freight service only. The depot still exists but is now used to house Traffic and Operations offices of the Southern Pacific Railroad. The depot remains as a reminder of the development of the area in bygone days when rail transport was of prime importance to Medford.

Menlo Park, California

Built by the first incorporated railroad in the state, Menlo Park depot is the oldest railroad depot still in use in California. In the 1850s, the area now known as Menlo Park, in San Mateo County, California, was being transformed from open grazing land to farm lands. Lots in the region had been purchased by Mr. Louis Golder in 1863, and in 1867 he sold a 100 by 720 foot strip of his land to the San Francisco and San Jose Railroad. On the acquired property this railroad built the wood-frame Menlo Park depot which was opened for traffic in August 1867. The company, that was to become the Southern Pacific, contracted to purchase the San Francisco and San Jose Railroad in 1868, and, by January 1870, the Menlo Park depot was the property of the expanding Southern Pacific Railroad company.

The coming of the railroad to the region also marked the development of the countryside for fashionable residential country estates that attracted many prominent citizens. The neat and trim little Menlo Park depot was often the place where carriages waited for distinguished visitors that included President Benjamin Harrison, General Ulysses S. Grant, and the Prince of Wales, later to become King Edward VII, who had come to visit other prominent residents of the area. Leland Stanford, Governor of California and, later, U.S. Senator, as well as many other prominent citizens, lived in the area over the years. In 1884 the Menlo Park depot had the first telephone exchange for the area, and four years later there were as many as ten subscribers to the service.

In addition to passenger service at the depot, old records show that all kinds of freight and merchandise were delivered there for area residents. Large amounts of fresh produce from the surrounding farms were also shipped from the depot to city markets, as the land in outlying areas was noted for its fertile soil that yielded a variety of produce.

The picturesque depot exhibited a variety of architectural styles — modified versions of the Queen Anne style, Victorian, Gothic, and Eastlake styles all hormoniously combined to form the resulting small, nineteenth-century building. The depot is basically of wood-frame construction with horizontal tongue-and-groove redwood siding. The gables at the north and south have decorative shingle siding, with doors and windows hooded with ornate drip-moulding trimmings. Simple ornamental brackets are found on the gable ends, with cornices above bay windows and eaves.

The depot, as originally built, was one story with attic, rectangular in plan, with a gabled roof on the north-south axis, a bay window on the south, and an additional steep gable in the center of the east side. The original all-redwood building had been enlarged in the 1870s by the addition of an ell at the southwest corner. In the 1880s the depot was updated

MENLO PARK, CALIFORNIA. An 1885 view of Menlo Park depot looking south down the line. This view shows the depot as originally built. Many prominent persons arrived and departed on trains from this depot in earlier times. Built in 1867, this depot still exists, but in its altered and expanded form. Note the roof-covered water tank at left and the long, wood-planked platform at right, fronting the depot. Carriages and people await the arrival of the train. *Southern Pacific.*

MENLO PARK, CALIFORNIA. A view of a passenger train at Menlo Park depot as it was in the 1890s. The depot still had its older, original, paint scheme, and there were some additions made to the building by this time. *Menlo Camera Shop Historical File.*

MENLO PARK, CALIFORNIA. Menlo Park depot as it looked about 1917, shortly after a new waiting-shed wing was added, as seen at right. Note that the wing is open, without end walls. The roof extension over the trackside bay window was also added at that time, with filler pieces added to the gabled ends of the roof. Note the benches with their multispaced armrests in front of the building and tree benches at left. *Menlo Camera Shop Historical File.*

with more decorative elements, including mouldings, brackets, and gable ornamentation. The extension, by 15 feet to the north of the main section of the building and another ell to the west, was done in the early 1890s. By 1917, a waiting shed at the north end was added to accommodate the increased service during World War I, due to the arrivals and departures of troops from nearby Camp Fremont.

Other alterations to the interior were made over the years, and in the spring of 1923 the Southern Pacific allotted over $5,000 for refurnishings of their station that included pavement and electric lights for the square occupied by the depot building, as part of the railroad's beautification program for the Menlo Park depot. Other alterations included forced-air heating system, linoleum installation on the floors, and suspended fluorescent lighting.

Since 1960, the depot has been used as the office of the Menlo Park Chamber of Commerce and as a commuter stop for trains, though it no longer serves as a ticket office. The depot still retains its picturesque, cottage style for its present use, though the interior was given additional minor alterations. The ladies' waiting room at the south end is now used as a conference room by the Chamber of Commerce and for civic group meetings, while still retaining its original, nineteenth-century character. This room is separated from the main lobby by a series of large glass ticket windows mounted on a structure of cabinets apparently part of the original interior furnishings. The main lobby was converted for secretarial-staff use, with

MENLO PARK, CALIFORNIA. A July 12. 1975 view of Menlo Park depot, showing its present architecture and with the additions of walls to the end waiting area at right. It is still a stop for commuter trains, but the main building portion is now the Menlo Park Chamber of Commerce. *Henry E. Bender, Jr.*

MENLO PARK, CALIFORNIA. The Menlo Park freight building is now used by a model railroad club and is located a few yards east of the depot. This July 1975 view shows the structure as it originally existed, although it was in need of some repairs. *Henry E. Bender, Jr.*

accoustical tile covering the ceiling and sheetrock panels over the original wall surfaces above the chair rail.

All of the alterations and additions made over the years reflect the growing and changing development of the community. The depot, now well over one hundred years old, and located approximately in the geographical center of Menlo Park, is a major landmark of the region. It remains as a terminus for hundreds of commuters on the daily trips to and from the San Francisco Peninsula, while continuing in its role as Chamber of Commerce and civic meeting place for the community.

The depot is still the property of the Southern Pacific and was listed in the National Register, with verification dated 1974. It is also on the State Historic Preservation Plan. The little Menlo Park depot remains a center of activity in good condition. It is significantly noted as the oldest railway station still in use in California.

Mount Clemens, Michigan

The Michigan Division of the Grand Trunk on the line of the railroad known as the Port Huron, Detroit and Chicago Branch, was completed in the autumn of 1859. The entire expense of construction and equipment was borne by the Grand Trunk Railroad Company of Canada. The Michigan Division enters Macomb County at the southwest corner of Richmond Township and traverses the county in a southwesterly direction. The Michigan Division was not opened until November 1859, and thus the Mount Clemens depot began service on the line that ran from Port Huron to Detroit Junction, a distance of fifty-nine miles.

It was on this Grand Trunk Division that the famous inventor, Thomas Alva Edison, began his career as a newspaper boy and candy butcher in the same year that the Michigan Division opened. Hired at the age of twelve, on this his first job, Edison worked from dawn to midnight on the Port Huron to Detroit run, using his spare time during layovers to experiment in a baggage-car chemistry laboratory. He moved his lab in 1862, after a phosphorous fire set the car ablaze, but substituted a printing press for his chemicals. He wrote and printed the first paper ever published on a moving train, *The Weekly Herald*, charging three cents a copy. Success was mixed with tragedy and heroism. An accident occurred while he was boarding a moving freight on the Port Huron run that left the young inventor partly deaf. In 1862, Edison's quick action saved the life of Jimmie Mackenzie, the three-year-old son of the Grand Trunk depot agent at Mount Clemens. Edison snatched the boy from the path of an oncoming train, and the grateful father, Mr. J. U. Mackenzie, an experienced telegrapher, rewarded Edison by offering to teach him to be a telegrapher. The fifteen-year-old lad accepted eagerly, and, to avail himself of the offer, he arranged to leave the car, with its printing press, at Mount Clemens, getting another newsboy to look after the Mount Clemens-Detroit portion of the trip. This was a turning point in the life of young Edison. The telegraph key on which he learned his craft is now in Greenfield Village Museum, Dearborne, Michigan. Edison was also an operator at the railroad's Stratford Junction, Ontario station, staying there until 1864.

The red-brick depot at Mount Clemens was believed to have been built by Findlay McDonald and his brother, both of whom built the Smith's Creek, Michigan, depot in 1858, and possibly others. The Mount Clemens depot, as it exists now, has had several revisions made to it since it was first built, but the basic structure is the same. The original chimneys are gone and several of the windows are bricked in. A large, folding-type door at left trackside of the depot was installed, replacing

MOUNT CLEMENS, MICHIGAN. The station was built in 1859 by the Grand Trunk Railway. This view of the Mount Clemens depot was taken in the winter of 1893, showing the building with its bay window, chimneys, and arched windows intact. *Grand Trunk Western.*

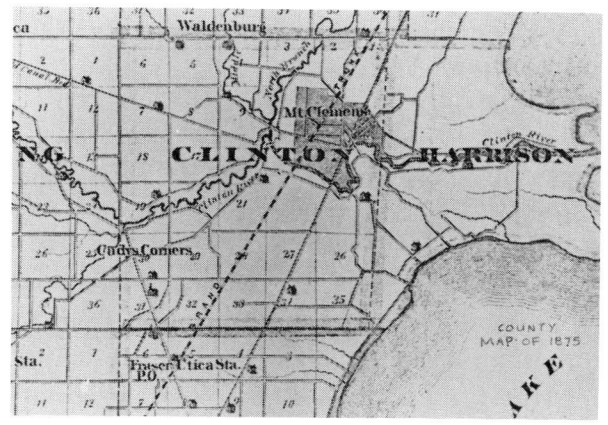

MOUNT CLEMENS, MICHIGAN. A portion of an 1875 county map showing the Mount Clemens area as it existed at that time. *Cavalier Collection.*

one of the windows, and there are several other changes of a minor nature as well. All windows and doors, arched in brick, with small circular vents for the attic, are located at both ends of the building above the windows. The original platform, also, no longer exists.

Original floor plans, dated October 2, 1917, indicate a bay window at trackside, some small rooms, and a garage at the rear of the depot, adjoining an unnamed dwelling. Lavatory rooms adjoining the main building, but not within it, were located to the left end of the depot as viewed from trackside. The floor plans also indicate revisions made on August 8, 1944, consisting of several major changes in the interior room arrangements and their uses, evidently made after the decline of passenger service at this depot. Of the original four chimneys, three are removed; the agent's bay window, all adjoining rooms not within the main building,

MOUNT CLEMENS, MICHIGAN. A front-right-end view of the depot, showing that much of the brickwork is still intact, as seen in this view of January 26, 1975. This view is comparable to the one taken in 1893, where similarities and changes to the architecture can be seen. *John Uckley.*

MOUNT CLEMENS, MICHIGAN. Looking down the line at the Mount Clemens depot. Note how the end door is set within the framing of the arched brickwork that is wider than the actual door. *John Uckley.*

MOUNT CLEMENS, MICHIGAN. This January 1975 view shows the depot's direct front elevation. The building is badly in need of repairs, as is evident from these more recent views. This depot is a historical site of the State of Michigan. *John Uckley.*

including the garage, lavatories, etc., are also removed. All interior rooms are completely revised and several windows bricked up. The floor plan drawings for both 1917 and 1944 with revisions show the comparisons.

The original 1859 Mount Clemens drawings could not be obtained and probably no longer exist. Additional revisions were also made in March and September of 1956, and again in February 1958.

Generally, the interior of the depot has changed completely from what originally existed. The floor plan of 1917 is almost the same as originally built. Perhaps the best comparison that can be made is with the old photograph of 1893 to those more recently taken in 1975.

It is interesting to note that at least three other Grand Trunk depots on the Michigan Division, all built the same year as Mount Clemens, are of almost identical design. These are at Fraser, Richmond, and New Haven, Michigan. These still show the agent's bay-window office area intact, as it once was in the Mount Clemens depot.

The all-brick depot at Mount Clemens is still structurally sound but does need some repairs, which should be done—especially considering it is now a Station Historical Site. A historical marker is posted within sight of the depot, marking it as a historical site of the State of Michigan, and recounts Edison's heroic deed of 1862.

Presently the Mount Clemens depot is being used by the Grand Trunk Western Railroad as an office for freight and a storehouse for maintenance equipment used on the line between Detroit and Port Huron. Though the depot may appear deserted, it is in use, offering some service to the railroad after well over one hundred years' existence.

MOUNT CLEMENS, MICHIGAN. An end-rear-corner view of the depot, showing where revisions to it had taken place at some time in the past. *John Uckley.*

MOUNT CLEMENS, MICHIGAN. A rear-corner view showing the curved braces of the roof overhang and end windows. Note the filled-in arches on the back wall. *John Uckley.*

Niles, Michigan

The Niles station is located in Berrien County, southwest Michigan, 190.6 miles west of Detroit on the Penn Central's Detroit-Chicago line. The station was built in 1891 by the Michigan Central Railroad, later the New York Central, now Penn Central. The building was constructed as a passenger station under the supervision of the railroad's Chief Engineer, J. D. Hawks. Ohio brown sandstone is used as the basic building material throughout the large building, which is approximately 190 feet in length, taking into account the baggage-express building at one end, but excluding roof-overhang widths. There are also a wing about 25 by 44 feet, projecting from the rear at one end of the main building, and a 68-foot-high clock tower with a large 5-foot-diameter clock dial.

The interior originally contained a large 46-foot-long waiting room at one end of the building, with the outer, end wall shaped like a semicircular, ten-window bay. Flanking this room at trackside is a small lobby and ticket office and, on the direct opposite rear side, another similar lobby and women's toilet room are located. Next to the ticket office at trackside is the small hall at the tower base, with steps leading up the tower. On the second floor of the tower a door leads to two adjoining, small rooms that comprise the operator's quarters, from which a small, bay window projects outward. These quarters are directly over the lobby and ticket office below. Next to the general waiting room is a smaller smoking room that opens onto the waiting room. The next room adjoining the smoking room is a large dining room with space for tables, and there is also a lunch counter in a horseshoe design within the same dining area. Directly off to the rear of the dining room is a preparation room and kitchen next to it, both of which make up the projected rear wing. Directly above this wing are several smaller rooms that make up the quarters for the restaurant manager and his family.

Most of the railroads with stations having dining rooms and other forms of restaurant facilities usually contract that part of the business to other companies who are responsible for that part of the facility, as well as for the quality of the food and health inspection. The railroads usually did not interfere with such establishments, as long as they met local standards and health requirements. It should be noted that not all large stations having restaurant facilities had living quarters as well for their restaurant staff or the management's family.

The Niles station is interesting in that it provided living quarters, indicating such business would be expected to warrant these architectural considerations. At the dining room end of the building a long corridor section connects the main building with the baggage-express room, a building 24 by 35 feet, that includes

NILES, MICHIGAN. Niles station as it looked on May 13, 1920. The building itself remains much the same today as it did when built in 1891. The grounds around the station are no longer kept up as they once were. *Official Railroad Photo, courtesy of C. R. Davidson.*

NILES, MICHIGAN. A front-left view of the station-tower portion with second-floor bay window. The posts and railings, at lower left in this view of August 4, 1974, are of a different design as compared with the 1920 view. *John Uckley.*

NILES, MICHIGAN. A front-right view of the station tower and entry. The photographer's father, Albert J. Uckley, poses near two of the doors that lead into the smoking room and dining room at right. *John Uckley.*

NILES, MICHIGAN. The second-story bay window and some of the various styles of window designs that are set deep in the Ohio-sandstone walls. *John Uckley.*

NILES, MICHIGAN. An end view, showing a portion of the rounded-end bay of the main general waiting room as it looked in August 1974. *John Uckley.*

NILES, MICHIGAN. An overall view of Niles station taken August 4, 1974, showing how grass and weeds have overgrown, uncontrolled, around the station. The building still appears to have its handsome style and qualities of Chateauesque influence. *John Uckley.*

NILES, MICHIGAN. An upward view of the clock tower with its five-foot dial clock. Fine-cut stonework is evident in this view, and the entire building is basically in good condition. *John Uckley.*

NILES, MICHIGAN. Originally built by the Michigan Central Railroad, this handsome structure, with interior use of plate and stained glass and brass ornamentation, was still in use when this photo was taken in 1974. *John Uckley.*

NILES, MICHIGAN. An unusual view of the Niles station, framed by a portion of a damaged freight car. The clock tower had been damaged by vandals, as seen in this 1975 view. Amtrak has allotted funds to renovate. *John Uckley.*

two small, adjoining toilet rooms at the rear side. The interior of the main building was tastefully decorated, making use of carved oak and light terra-cotta in the walls and ceilings, as well as plate and stained glass in the windows.

The exterior of this handsome building has multileveled roofs of various styles, including rounded sloping bay, hipped, as well as dormers, and a pyramid-styled roof on the tower. Windows also varied in style and design that included the broad-arched window of the dining room at trackside. In general, there is a quality of Chateauesque influence to the building, with the tower being a most outstanding architectural feature.

Originally, the grounds were laid out with attractive landscaping that featured exquisite flower beds, manicured lawns, and various types of trees and shrubbery, as well as a fish pond and park benches. The station was literally a place where local citizens could visit and relax in those early times and perhaps take a leisurely stroll, a common thing for families to do on a Sunday afternoon.

The station still exists and is in active railroad service today, though there was some concern for its future at one time. Evidently the station is still considered important by the railroad because Amtrak recently installed a ticket agent there and spent $70,000 to spruce up the old building, which was sadly neglected for many years. The Niles station remains as a fine example of late-nineteenth-century railroad-station architecture executed in stone and is certainly worthy of preservation.

North Conway, New Hampshire

The ornate Victorian passenger station at North Conway, New Hampshire, was built in 1874 by the Portsmouth, Great Falls and Conway Railroad. In 1878, this railroad was leased to the Eastern Railroad, which was acquired in 1890 by the Boston and Maine Railroad. The station is located 137 miles north of Boston at the south entrance to the White Mountain region.

It is believed that the North Conway station was designed and built by Nathaniel J. Bradlee, an architect by profession, who was born in Boston on June 1, 1829, and died while on a business trip in Vermont on December 17, 1888. Mr. Bradlee was a very active man and quite prominent in Boston where he lived. He had designed a large number of buildings, including the Union Station at Portland, Maine, which has now been razed. He was director of numerous companies, including the Boston and Maine Railroad, and Maine Central Railroad, as well as president of several other nonrailroad companies. This information is acknowledged by Mr. David B. Childs, grandson of Mr. Bradlee, in a communication to Carroll P. Reed. He and William Levy are the present owners of the North Conway station building.

The North Conway station design is perhaps one of the most interesting and unique in America for its style. The building is basically of wood-frame construction, two stories high, with large, twin towers placed at opposite ends of the main building block, and with a central-roof-cupola section. The design is generally symmetrical about the shorter center axis, with a canopy-shelter roof surrounding the building just above the first-floor windows and doors. Both end towers, about 27 by 11½ feet in size, project outward about 6 feet to one side of the main building block, and there is a wide, centrally located bay window on the other side. A single brick chimney is set on the center of the cupola, and round dial clocks, centered within curved dormers, are set within larger curved-dormer projections.

The twin towers are perhaps the most significant features of the design, with their curved and sloping roof styles. Older photo views reveal small, circular windows located on all sides of the broad curve of the lower tower roofs. The tower windows are arched in contrast to the rectangular windows of the lower floor, which have hoods over them, as do the entry doors. Horizontal siding covers the exterior walls, with tin and shingles covering the various roof levels. The skirting canopy extends out about 9 feet and is supported by

NORTH CONWAY, NEW HAMPSHIRE. An early view of North Conway station, taken about 1875, with a southbound train stopped at the station. Note the diamond pattern on the sloping tower roof and frilled trimming around the first-floor canopy shelter, both of which do not exist now. The wood-burning locomotive and train is of the Portsmouth, Great Falls and Conway Railroad (Eastern Railroad). *Collection of Conway Scenic Railroad, Inc.*

NORTH CONWAY, NEW HAMPSHIRE. An 1886 view of North Conway station, showing the small, dome-roof, circular windows that no longer exist. A number of horse drawn carriages await the arrival of the train. *Walker Transportation Collection—Beverly, Mass. Historical Society.*

NORTH CONWAY, NEW HAMPSHIRE. This 1911 view shows a platform canopy shelter not seen in the earlier views. New fencing has also been installed, and the station has been repainted. The long, trackside, platform shelter was later removed. *Harold K. Vollrath Collection.*

NORTH CONWAY, NEW HAMPSHIRE. A trackside view of the station as it looked in September 1959 while still in active service for the Boston and Maine Railroad. *Walker Transportation Collection—Beverly, Mass. Historical Society.*

NORTH CONWAY, NEW HAMPSHIRE. A 1961 trackside view of the station, taken the same year the Boston & Maine Railroad ceased running passenger trains to North Conway. Two years later the railroad sold the station to Eliot Realty Company. *Walker Transportation Collection—Beverly, Mass. Historical Society.*

North Conway station as it looked in August 1974 and was used by the Conway Scenic Railroad, Inc. The building is brightly colored in yellow with white trim, black roof, and a new sign hanging from the lower eave at center. An excellent example of restoration and reuse of a railroad station as an operating facility, as well as the preservation of a unique style of railroad station architecture. *Bradley Peters Photo.*

carved columns, each having smaller carved braces adjoining the canopy underside. Large triangular braces also support the canopy in pairs around the building, adjoining it and the canopy. Delicate, ornate, iron ridging tops the towers and the main roof sections between the center cupola and towers.

The first floor originally contained large, separate, men's and women's waiting rooms, each having a corner staircase that gave access to the upper floor. A ticket office was next to the bay-window area, with ticket windows facing both of the waiting rooms. One tower first-floor room was used as a baggage room and the other, next to the women's waiting room, was used in part as a women's toilet room, with a slightly smaller portion as the men's toilet that had a separate, outside-entry door. The overall length of the building, excluding roof overhangs, is about 100 by 37 feet and includes the bay window and tower protrusions, with overall height to the top of the towers being about 52 feet.

There was once a long, canopied, open, platform shelter, seen in the 1911 photograph, that was erected in 1898, but later removed. When originally built, no such canopy was constructed. In 1908 a new floor was installed in the ticket office, and a year earlier the building had been reshingled. In 1912 both the interior and the exterior were repainted.

The Boston and Maine Railroad altered the interior rooms of the station in the early 1920s. The men's toilet room was converted into a storeroom and the women's toilet room was partitioned off to make smaller, men's and women's toilet rooms. The south end of the men's waiting room, next to the baggage room, was partitioned off for use by the Railway Express Agency. The northwest corner of the men's waiting room was partitioned off and converted into a furnace room.

In 1961 the Boston and Maine ceased running passenger trains to North Conway, and their very last freight train departed from the closed station in October 1972. In July 1963, the Boston and Maine sold the station to Eliot Realty Company. In May 1965, Eliot Realty sold the station to Messrs. William Levy and Carroll P. Reed to form a North Conway Depot Company. On May 24, 1974, the two station owners deeded the station to the Conway Scenic Railroad, Inc. The owners of the Conway Scenic Railroad are Mr. Reed, Mr. Levy, and Mr. Dwight Smith.

In 1974 the Conway Scenic Railroad made some alterations to the station in an effort to restore it to its original character. They did away with the storeroom and rebuilt the two toilet rooms completely, making modern men's and ladies' facilities in the 12-by-27 foot area originally used for this purpose. The furnace room was removed, as was the partition for the express office in the men's waiting room. A large opening was cut into the north wall of the ticket office where the CSRR now has its ticket counter. The old ticket windows in the east and south walls of the ticket office have been left intact.

New uses were also made of some of the rooms. The women's waiting room is now the CSRR museum, the men's waiting room is now the CSRR Brass Whistle Gift Shop, and the baggage room is now occupied by the CSRR Flag Stop Snack Bar. The room on the south end of the second floor is now occupied by the HO layout of the North Conway Depot Model Railroad Club. The room at the north end of the second floor is used by the CSRR as a storeroom. Physically, the interior of the station looks almost as it did when built, except for the addition of early style incandescent lighting. The building's exterior was given a new painting, with bright colors of yellow, white trimming, and red over the tin portions of the roofs, which makes the structure stand out well, clearly showing its architectural features.

The station exists today in excellent condition and is in active use, serving as the base of operations for the Conway Scenic Railroad's eleven-mile train ride with steam-operated locomotive and passenger cars. One hundred years have passed since the station was built and restored in its centennial year. It certainly is worth visiting this unique station, a very fine example of late-nineteenth-century railroad-station architecture in the United States, and certainly a credit to North Conway.

North Easton, Massachusetts

The first railroad in Easton, Massachusetts, was owned and built by the Easton Branch Railroad Company in 1854. The international shovel industry was centered in Easton at that time, and this product was produced by the Oliver Ames and Sons Company. One of the primary functions of the railroad, and its main reason for having been built here, was for the transportation of shovels from the plant at Easton to various markets. The Shovel Works was founded in 1803 by Oliver Ames, and, by mid-century, it had become the world's largest shovel factory, due to the great increasing need for this product for expanding construction and the discovery of gold in California, Australia, and other places.

The railroad eventually became part of the Old Colony Railroad system in 1866, and, in November 1881, the vice-president of the Old Colony, Frederick L. Ames, who was a friend and patron of architect Henry H. Richardson, commissioned him to design the station building which is now at North Easton. This handsome building was one of five significant, still-surviving buildings Richardson had designed for the Ames family. In 1882, the station building was given by Mr. Ames to the Old Colony Railroad, later to become part of the New York, New Haven, and Hartford Railroad,

NORTH EASTON, MASSACHUSETTS. The North Easton station as it looked in 1890. Note the continued roof extensions of the canopy shelter on both ends of the building. These shelters have long since been removed. *Courtesy Easton Historical Society.*

of which the Ames family were principal stockholders.

The station building is basically constructed of cut granite set on a low, red-sandstone base, with a broad course of the same red sandstone encircling the building at about mid-point on the exterior walls. Two deep-set, wide arches of similar design with red- sandstone, radius courses are located on both sides of the building and extend from the base arching high around the wall facades. These arches are a main source of light as they each contain

NORTH EASTON, MASSACHUSETTS. An 1890 view of the rear-portico cochere of the station. Passengers arrived and departed from here in horse-drawn vehicles. The broad arches are like those on the opposite side of the building. *Courtesy Easton Historical Society.*

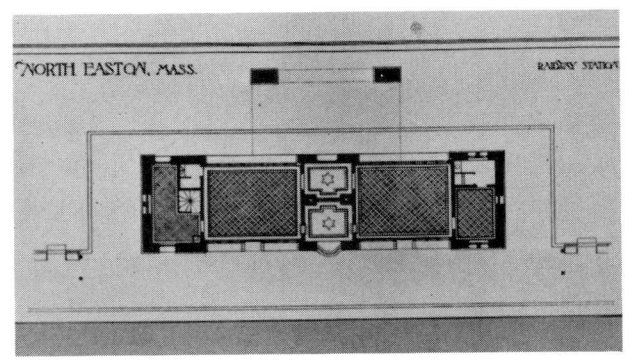

NORTH EASTON, MASSACHUSETTS. The floor plan of the North Easton station as designed by Henry H. Richardson, showing the first-floor room arrangements with ticket office in center flanked by two waiting rooms. *Photo: The Oaks Ames Memorial Hall Association and The Easton Historical Society.*

several windows at either side and above a centrally positioned entry door. Deep-set, double windows are also located outside the arched areas at either end, separated by a stone mullion in each set of these windows. There is a single window centered on the north, end wall and a single, wide door centered on the south, end wall.

A wide, overhanging, hip roof covers the building, with two wide dormers on the west slope of the roof, each having a row of five windows. The roof overhang is supported by large, triangular-shaped braces set in pairs on the end walls and in wider pairs on the side, with their bases set on stone corbels. At the east rear side of the building is a centrally located porte cochere. This also has a hip roof and a broad arch spanning two granite pillars that support the roof extension. A single chimney, made of smaller cut stones, is centrally located on the roof peak.

Richardson was an architect who took great care in his building designs and was particular about much of the detail and decorative configurations he designed for them. In the case of the North Easton station, he used two boar heads carved in the supporting beams opposite one another under the overhang junction of the main roof and porte cochere. Boar heads are also carved in the window lintels of the arches on this same east side, two for each arch. On the west side of the station, flanking the entry doors, are sets of outside benches, with lion heads carved in the arm rests.

The station's interior contained two waiting rooms, a centrally located ticket office, and a baggage room at the building's north end. The small, bay window at trackside extends from the ticket office. The station originally had a long, open-platform, canopy shelter along trackside that extended out from both ends of the building. This is seen in one of the 1890 photo views pictured here, but this part of the structure no longer exists.

The station continued in service until June 1959, when the Old Colony Branch ceased operations, and the station building was closed up and left abandoned. It remained in this vacant state for over ten years, during which time it deteriorated, though it was still structurally sound—especially in the stone work. As the New York, New Haven, and Hartford Railroad was facing bankruptcy at the time, efforts were made to secure sources for new funds—partly through the sale of its abandoned railroad stations, of which North Easton was one.

In 1966, the Easton Historical Society started to function once again, after a dormant eighteen years, and developed from a small core of in-

NORTH EASTON, MASSACHUSETTS. A July 1970 view of the North Easton station. Much of the building has since been restored by the Easton Historical Society after the station had been closed for over ten years. *Courtesy Easton Historical Society.*

NORTH EASTON, MASSACHUSETTS. A more recent view of the North Easton station, taken March 1976. Much restoration had already been accomplished by the Easton Historical Society by the time this photo was taken. *Courtesy Easton Historical Society.*

terested people into a small but flourishing organization. The Society made known to the community its desire to secure the North Easton station building for its headquarters building and museum. Late in 1969, the Society was joyfully surprised to learn that the station building property they wanted was to be given to the Society as a gift from Mr. William A. Parker, Mr. John S. Ames, Jr., Mr. David Ames, and Senator Oliver F. Ames, who had secured the deed to the property after negotiating its purchase from the railroad.

Almost immediately, work commenced on the restoration of the station building, which, in the beginning stages, was a community project. To start, the boards were removed from windows and doors, refuse cleared away, and some 120 glass panes were replaced in the windows of this historical station. It was the last remaining example of small-station building architecture designed by the famous H. H. Richardson. Since the initial restoration began, many additional funds and hours of work, as well as research for information and documents to be used as a basis for the progressive steps of restoration, were put into the continued efforts of this project by members of the Society.

On March 28, 1970, the building started in its new role as the Easton Historical Society headquarters and museum. Future renovations are to be made in the second floor, possibly for a curator's apartment and/or as storage for artifacts and library facilities. The large cellar area will also be renovated as an additional display area for artifacts that are also on display in the first-floor-south-waiting-room area. The station is now open to the public on the first Sunday of each month from 2:00 P.M.to 4:00 P.M.

The North Easton station was placed on the National Register of Historic Places, with verification dated 1972. The building remains as a very fine example of Romanesque style of railroad-station architecture still in use today, is important for its role in the early development of the community, and is certainly a credit to it.

Oradell, New Jersey

The Oradell depot is located in Bergen County, New Jersey, 17.9 miles north of Jersey City in the northeastern corner of the state and west of the Hudson River. The depot, built in 1890 by the New Jersey and New York Railroad, was then situated at the end of the railroad's double track. The station agent at that time was Mr. Earnest E. Hinds, and, since the depot was a train-register point, its telegraph was constantly busy.

The original Oradell depot still existed in 1890 when the new depot was built and was located directly across the tracks from the new building. The older depot was a smaller, single-story, wood-frame depot, rectangular in shape with vertical board and batten exterior walls. The depot had few windows, and skirting around it was an overhang roof shelter supported by a series of long, shallow-arched, wood supports, above which the exterior wall projected a short distance to the roof. About center on the low roof was a square cupola with air vents on all sides and topped with a small pyramid-type sloping roof with an old-style weather vane projecting from its center peak. This old depot was relocated in 1891 to a site about 100 yards north of the new depot and converted for use as a freight house. It was placed on slightly higher ground, and a raised wood platform on level with the depot floor was added directly at trackside, so as to be on a level with freight car floors for easier transfer of freight.

The new Oradell depot is a much larger and more elaborate building than the old depot. It is one-and-one-half stories, or single story with usable attic space, generally rectangular in shape with a seven-foot-wide porch that surrounds the 16-by-40-foot main building. The building is of wood-frame construction, has a bay window at trackside, and the exterior walls are covered with decorative shingles. The depot and its porch are on a slightly higher level than the tracks. Originally, a wide set of steps went up to the porch from ground level at trackside and were located directly in front of the bay-windowed ticket office. These steps have since been replaced with narrower steps and railing in the same center location.

The rear of the building originally had a porte cochere where carriages brought and picked up passengers. The main building is symmetrical in design about its shorter axis, with multigabled roofs, and a small, central, square, building portion juts slightly above the main roof center with an octagonal, pyramid-shaped roof topping it. From this central portion, short, gabled-roof dormers project on both sides of the shorter axis, while two other longer, gabled roofs extend from it on either end on the longer major axis. The main building roof extends down from the lower gables at both ends

ORADELL, NEW JERSEY. A trackside view of the Oradell depot taken in July 1974. The building looks much the same as it did when built in 1890 in this frontal view. It had replaced a smaller wood-frame depot that was originally located directly across the tracks. *Herbert H. Harwood, Jr.*

ORADELL, NEW JERSEY. The Oradell station is no longer used for passenger service but is reused as the Cricket Gift Shop. The area fronting the depot is still a train stop, as seen in this view of July 1974. *Herbert H. Harwood, Jr.*

ORADELL, NEW JERSEY. An end view of the depot shows that the porte cochere no longer exists at left in this view looking north and taken in 1970. The open-porch area is reminiscent of residential homes of the period. Note the sloping access doors at lower left to the lower level under the building. *Don P. Wallworth Photo, Collection of Herbert H. Harwood, Jr.*

and continues from these two gables on either side of the longer axis, resulting in the extended, roof overhang around the entire building. The overhang is supported at regular intervals by carved-wood columns that are connected by railings along the trackside porch frontage at one end. The dormer and gabled ends have narrow, rectangular window frames with small stained-glass windows that are also found in the square upper portion on all sides. The roof peaks originally had upper ornate-designed ridging that no longer exists.

Adjoining the main building at one end is a smaller 16-by-20-foot single-room attached structure whose roof joins the roof of the main building. This attachment is on ground level, having a large, freight door on both sides and two windows at the ends. The main roof overhang next to this attachment and porch below created an open breezeway between the main building end wall and the wall of the attached single-room building. This attachment appears to have been an addition to the main building, as it is self-contained and believed to have been added immediately after the main building was constructed. Old floor plans reveal that it was used as a Wells Fargo Express Office and was probably added for this purpose.

The main building originally had one large full-length waiting room with a ticket office and a small storage room, both centrally located opposite each other. Both rooms projected inward into the waiting room so as to form a

ORADELL, NEW JERSEY. A closer view of the front-track side-porch facade, showing detail of the porch, tower, dormer, and stairway, as it looked in July 1974. The building appears to be in good overall condition. *Herbert H. Harwood, Jr.*

5-foot-wide corridor at the center. This created a men's waiting room adjacent to the Wells Fargo Express Office and a women's waiting room at the opposite end. The ceiling was 16-feet high, and seating benches were located at both ends and along both side walls, terminating at the entry doors. There were four entry doors to the waiting rooms, two on each side wall, flanking both the ticket office and the storage room. A fifth entry door was centered on the rear wall for outside access to the storage room. There were outside steps leading under the building at one end and toilet facilities in a detached, small, six-by-ten-foot outhouse, both items being located at the opposite end of the Wells Fargo office. The outhouse was about 30 feet from the end of the building and had a high fence around it. A partition separated the men's and women's toilets, and both toilets had separate entry doors located on the opposite end walls of this little structure.

Interior alterations were made to the main building after 1913. The small storage room was removed and small lavatory rooms for men and women installed in the same area, occupying an overall space of 5 by 15 feet. The exterior door to the storeroom was sealed off, and two exterior windows, one for each toilet room, were installed, flanking the original exterior, covered-door location. At some time in the past, the elegant porte cochere at the rear of the depot was removed, and windows in the small, roof-gabled ends and dormers closed off.

The New Jersey and New York Railroad was once a subsidiary of the then Erie Railroad. The Erie was subsequently merged and became the Erie Lackawanna Railway, which presently operates the line. Today the building is no longer used as a passenger station but exists in good condition as the Cricket Gift Shop. The building is painted a now-fading yellowish color with dark green railings and roof trimmings.

The Oradell depot is still a train stop for limited commuter service, but the building has no agent or waiting room facilities. Passengers wait outside on the porch or area fronting the tracks. Except for the removal of the rear porte cochere, the depot's appearance remains essentially the same. The building exists as a fine example of late-nineteenth-century Victorian railroad-station architecture and has much of its original character.

Perris, California

The Perris station is located eighteen miles from Highgrove on the Atchison, Topeka & Santa Fe's Highgrove and Jacinto line in west Riverside County, southern California. The station was built in late 1891 for the Southern California Railway, a wholly owned subsidiary of the Atchison, Topeka & Santa Fe Railroad Company. The Southern California Railway Company, as it was first called before the station was built, began constructing a railroad north from San Diego and National City in 1881. By April 1882 it was complete as far as a small settlement known as Pinacate, which became a supply center for the local gold mines, with a station consisting of a box car on a rail siding. By September 13, 1883, through service from National City to San Bernardino was in operation, and on November 15, 1885, through transcontinental train service from Chicago via the Santa Fe to San Diego passed through Pinacate.

In 1885 a dispute occurred between the railroad and local land owners that resulted in the railroad's relocating the depot site about a mile north and renaming it Perris, in honor of Fred T. Perris, who was the Chief Engineer of the Southern California at that time. Perris also became a junction point for the new branch line to Hemet and San Jacinto, and a branch line to the small community of Lakeview. At this time a wood-frame building served as the depot, but the townspeople wanted a better building. After 1888 Perris was no longer on the main line when a Santa Fe subsidiary built through lines between San Bernardino and Los Angeles and between Los Angeles and San Diego, but construction began anyway on one of the grandest station buildings a small town could ever hope for. By the time the building was completed, disastrous floods in Temecula Canyon, thirty miles south of Perris, had cut the through line to San Diego, and the station building ended up serving an unimportant branch line. The last trains to San Diego ran in February 1891; thereafter, traffic on the branch, mostly carrying seasonal farm products, continued to decline.

In 1927 construction of a dam ten miles south of Perris caused the railroad to abandon service to the south towards Elsinore, and trains were rerouted through Corona. Perris was now a way point on the San Jacinto branch, and passenger service was reduced drastically to a single coach on a mixed train, which was also eventually discontinued in 1953. In the 1960s special trains run by the Orange Empire Railway Museum passed the Perris station on their way to the famous Ramona Pageant at Hemet. A few years before the advent of Amtrak, the expense of these trips became excessive and the railroad's reluctance

PERRIS, CALIFORNIA. Looking towards the baggage-room end of the Perris station as a train leaves the brick-constructed structure, which was built in 1891. The station exists today, housing displays of local history. Note the low, freight door at left. *Joe Garnand Photo, courtesy Orange Empire Railway Museum.*

PERRIS, CALIFORNIA. An Orange Empire Railway Museum-sponsored special train preparing to leave the Perris station for the Ramona Pageant in Hemet on April 20, 1963. *William Bassler Photo, courtesy Orange Empire Railway Museum.*

PERRIS, CALIFORNIA. Perris station was built for the Southern California Railway, a wholly owned subsidiary of the Atchison, Topeka and Santa Fe Railway Company. The sloping brickwork and faded-line shape on the wall at right, fronting the open freight door, gives some evidence that a freight platform may have existed there at one time. *Santa Fe Railway Photo.*

PERRIS, CALIFORNIA. A twin-window design, showing detail in the window-pane pattern. The single-bay windows are similar but with only two vertical panels in the lower frame. *William T. Wootton.*

SAN JUAN CAPISTRANO, CALIFORNIA. Built in 1895, the San Juan Capistrano station building is a fine example of early attempts in the revival of the California Mission style of architecture. This view of August 12, 1968, shows the station as it looked when service was discontinued that same year and prior to renovations to it for its conversion as a depot restaurant. *Henry E. Bender, Jr.*

MOUNT CLEMENS, MICHIGAN. There have been considerable alterations made to the Mount Clemens station since it was first built in 1859, although the basic structure's exterior still remains, but greatly modified. The station is famous for its association with Thomas Alva Edison. The building is still used by the Grand Trunk Western and is a State Historical Site, as seen in this view of January 1975. *John Uckley.*

to use branch lines combined to end the last passenger service the branch will most likely ever see.

Today, the Orange Empire Railway Museum sits on the exact site of that old western town of Pinacate, of which one tiny storage building remains. The current owner of the Perris station building is the Orange Empire Railway Museum, Inc., of Perris, California. The station had continued in service until it closed on December 11, 1969. It was officially turned over to the Orange Empire Trolley Museum in a special ceremony on October 2, 1971. Although the museum owns the station building, the land it sits on, as well as surrounding lands, is still owned by the Santa Fe.

The station building is a combination passenger and freight design of brick construction, generally of a rectangular shape in plan, with various roof styles and a handsome two-story tower. The interior contains a large, freight room at one end, with three freight doors whose base height is on a level with the raised floor within. Small circular windows at the end and side walls are found in the upper freight room walls. Next to this room is a small, freight office at the rear side and a smaller open entry directly opposite at trackside next to the

PERRIS, CALIFORNIA. A front trackside view of the station as it looked on August 7, 1976. The conical-roofed open tower is a prominent feature of the station. *William T. Wootton.*

131

PERRIS, CALIFORNIA. A rear trackside view of the station taken August 1976, showing the freight-end portion and small open platform. Note the small circular windows on the ends and side just under the roof overhang. Much of the trimmings and ornate roof cresting remain intact. *William T. Wootton.*

tower. This entry opens to the ticket office with rounded bay, and directly behind it at the rear is another open entry. That entry opens to the freight office, ticket office, and waiting room adjoining the ticket office, which also has an entry door at trackside. Next to the waiting room at the end is a small, baggage room with three wide doors—a smaller one at the end and one large door on each side.

The higher central portion of the building has its roof at right angles to the main axis with one wing on either side, a hipped roof over the freight room, and a gabled hipped end roof over the other. A high, conical roof tops the open tower and is supported by a series of small, carved columns that are connected by arched lattice work in their upper portions. The two broad-arched entry ways, one on each side of the building, are of similar design. The doorways all have brick voussoirs, and brick-designed trimmings are evident in several places throughout the exterior walls and in the gabled ends of the upper-roof portions. Windows are mainly rectangular, with multipaned upper sash and with similar designs in the entry door windows. The design and attention to the architectural detail is evident throughout the entire building and is, surprisingly, quite elaborate and attractive for a small-town railroad station.

In 1975 two of the four tracks in the station

yard were abandoned, leaving only one siding to the east and the main line to the west of the depot. Freight on the branch today is still mostly agricultural. The agent closest to Perris is at the March Air Force Base depot, a classic old depot building twelve miles northwest of Perris.

The Perris station stands today basically as it was in the 1890s, except that in later years a Swift train-order signal was added on the west side, plus an air conditioner. The interior is generally the same, except for modern facilities in the restrooms of the former waiting room. Other changes include gingerbread trim extended along the uppermost roof peak on the north office portion of the building. A large sign reading: "SANTA FE ROUTE" was fixed exactly halfway along the roof peak between the north side of the building and where the roof connects with the portion containing the tower.

The Perris station building currently houses a small museum staffed by volunteers from the Perris area. There are plans to replace missing furniture in the ticket office, thus restoring the station in this respect to its appearance in passenger-carrying days of the 1920s. This will not involve any structural changes at this time.

The museum is essentially one of valley history and momentos and is open to the public without admission cost. No alterations to the station's interior structure were made for the museum, and none are planned for the future. The Perris station, in excellent condition, remains in use today and is a fine example of brick, railroad-station architecture of the late nineteenth century.

Pewee Valley, Kentucky

The Pewee Valley station was located in Jefferson County, Kentucky, about sixteen miles northeast of the city of Louisville, very close to the Indiana state line on the east bank of the Ohio River. The station building was built in 1867 by the Louisville & Frankfort Railroad as a combination station in the small suburban community that is largely residential. It served a heavy volume of daily passenger traffic, especially in the summer months when affluent Louisville residents commuted to their summer homes located in the cooler and higher areas of Pewee Valley. The scene at the new station upon the arrival of the first train in 1867 was recorded in the photograph presented here. Several dozen of the local residents greeted the passenger train on that opening day long ago as it rolled into the impressive and important-looking station. It was the only station built there, was meant to be an outstanding building to impress Louisville's elite, and added a measure of importance to the village. In 1881 the Louisville & Frankfort became part of the Louisville & Nashville Railroad, and the Pewee Valley station continued in its undisturbed service and was a very active center for many years.

The station building was basically a rectangular, two-story structure, with a cement platform that surrounded the entire building. At trackside the platform extended out from the building 22½ feet across the full length of the building and continued out on either end along the tracks at a 10-foot width for 94 feet at one end and 103 feet along the other end. Adjacent to the building ends and rear, the platform was 6 feet wide, and short flights of steps led down from the upper main platform area to the slightly lower level of the ends and rear areas. The rear of the building had three entry doors, each with short flights of steps leading down to the rear-platform walkway.

The building was basically of brick construction with strip-layed tin roofing. The main gabled roof was centered on the longitudinal axis with three gabled roofs at right angles to it. The central gable was larger than the other two that flanked it and had three shallow-arched windows in the gabled end, while only one centered window was in each of the other two smaller gabled ends. All gabled ends had ornamented, carved trimmings within the inner slope of the roofs. Centered on the peak of the main roof was a small, attractive-looking octagonally shaped cupola with arched louvered vents in every other side wall and topped with an octagonal, cone-shaped roof with an iron weather vane extending up from it. Brick chimneys were also centered on the roof peak, one at the baggage room area, and one on either side of the roof's cupola, which was used mainly for ventilation of the attic space above the second floor. A tin roof-covered platform canopy with decorative eave trimmings skirted

PEWEE VALLEY, KENTUCKY. Pewee Valley station was built in 1867 by the Louisville and Frankfort Railroad as a combination station for a small residential community. The station continued in service until it was closed and demolished in 1960. This early photo shows the grand opening of the station in 1867 as the train arrived. It stopped to pose along with a number of citizens who had gathered along the platform to greet the train on that important day long ago. *Louisville and Nashville Public Relations.*

PEWEE VALLEY, KENTUCKY. A 1951 view of Pewee Valley station. The building looks basically much the same as when built, except that much of the original trimmings no longer exist along the roof overhangs. *Boyce F. Martin Photo.*

the building just above the first-floor windows and was supported by triangular-shaped curved braces. A small, bay window was on the first floor, located just to the left of center at track side.

The first floor of the interior contained a ladies' waiting room at one end to the left of the bay window, with a small toilet room adjoining it. Next to this was a narrow-shaped agent's office from which the bay windows projected, and adjoining it a large, centrally located general waiting room. The agent's office had ticket windows that opened to both of the waiting rooms that flanked it. Next to the general waiting room was the baggage room, and within this room, against the general waiting-room wall, was a separate stairway leading up to the second floor, with a separate entry door to the rear of the building. On both sides of the building are entry doors from the ladies' waiting room, general waiting room, and baggage room, with no steps at the rear baggage-room door but with steps at the rear from the other doors.

Steps up to the second floor led to a 6-foot-wide hallway located along the trackside part of the building. This hallway ended in a large chamber at one end over the lower, ladies'

PEWEE VALLEY, KENTUCKY. Pewee Valley station in 1952, showing the Louisville and Nashville's "Pan American" train picking up mail on the fly as it heads northbound from Louisville to Cincinatti. *Boyce F. Martin Photo.*

waiting room. Doors to two other slightly smaller rooms centrally located opened to the hallway, and at the other end was another chamber with a smaller adjoining room. Two of the rooms had closets, and all rooms and the hallway had windows. The chamber next to the stairway had a fireplace, and although all the second-floor rooms are not labeled on the 1867 floor plans, it is believed the second floor was used as the agent's living quarters. Ceiling heights of the first floor were eleven feet, and there were basement rooms under the baggage room and ladies' waiting room at the opposite end of the building. Overall size of the building was approximately 80 by 27 feet.

The station continued in its service well into the present twentieth century. Some minor alterations had been made, such as the removal of the ornate roof trimmings in later years, but with no other outstanding revisions. After ninety-three years of service, the station was closed and eventually demolished in 1960. It had changed very little since it was built, up to the time it was razed. No replacement agency or mobile van service is offered there now, the nearest agency being a yard office at O'Bannon, Kentucky, the next station south on the line. The community still remains largely residential with no industry. The Pewee Valley station was a fine example of suburban mid-nineteenth-century railroad-station architecture of the post-Civil War period—of which very few station buildings still survive.

Point of Rocks, Maryland

The Baltimore and Ohio Railroad's station at Point of Rocks, in Frederick County, Maryland, is located forty-two miles west of Camden station in Baltimore on the Baltimore to Cumberland main line. In the early 1830s, the Baltimore and Ohio Railroad was constructing its route west of the Ohio River as was the Chesapeake and Ohio Canal. As both chose a route westward from Point of Rocks along a narrow corridor of land between the Potomac River and the Catoctin Mountains, a conflict arose. The Maryland Court of Appeals solved the suit by allowing both parties to share and proceed along the narrow corridor of land that both had wished to use.

The Baltimore and Ohio Railroad selected Mr. E. Francis Baldwin of Baltimore to head their architectural department in the mid-1870s. It is believed that Mr. Baldwin designed the Point of Rocks station, which was built in 1875, the same time his design of the railroad's headquarters building was built in Baltimore. The importance of the railroad at that time, especially with regard to small towns, is indicated by the present site of the town, which had moved to this location to be near the railroad's track route that connected with the cities of Washington, DC, and Baltimore to the east, and all points on the mainline westward from Point of Rocks.

The station building is designed in the Gothic-Revival style. Its overall plan is shaped somewhat like a stubbed *T*, two stories high, with a tower projecting above at one end and a single-story wing with attic crossing it at right angles at the other end. The tower is a significant feature of the building, rising approximately four stories high, with attic space in the third story and with dormer windows on three sides. Above these is the narrow square portion of the tower on which a small pyramidal roof, laced with cut-wood decorative trimmings, is located.

The central two-story section has a hip roof with a pair of smaller dormers, one having gabled roof and the other hip roof, which adds variety and interest to the deisgn. Two porches project from each side of this central section, with carved supporting brackets. The building is of red-brick construction with distinctive bands of light granite running horizontally at the base, below the first-story window sills, and a third below the sills of the second-story windows—all on the main block of the building only. Most of the windows and doors of the main block have lintels that join the middle, light-granite band, forming a continuing effect in this trim line. The overall effect of these trimmings and the numerous other details found throughout the building's exterior add much to the entire Gothic style and elaborate architecture of the station.

POINT OF ROCKS, MARYLAND. The Point of Rocks Station was Built in 1875 by the Baltimore and Ohio Railroad. This view shows the station as it looked in 1950 in its general setting in relation to the tracks. The station looks much the same today as it did when built over one hundred years ago. *C. L. Andrews Photo.*

The first floor contained a large waiting room with two separate entry doors at one end and an adjoining, women's toilet room centered between an express room and men's toilet room. Both of these had access by entry doors on the outside in order to isolate them from the main large waiting room. A single staircase near one corner of this room gives access to the upper floors. These rooms were contained within the winged one-and-one-half-story portion of the building. Adjoining the main waiting room was another smaller waiting room, a ticket office, agent's room, and a baggage room. All of these rooms were contained within the main two-story block of the first floor. The second floor of the main block, entered by the stairway from the main waiting room, led to a central corridor that gave access to five additional rooms. Over the portion of the one-and-one-half-story wing was a centrally located single room with access doors on opposite walls leading to large attic spaces at both ends and flanking the one central room.

The station continued in its service for many years without hazardous incident until 1931 when lightning struck the building. This jolt caused serious damage to the roof and second floor, which were destroyed by fire resulting from this unexpected force of nature. Charles W. Galloway, then the Vice-president of Operations, ordered the damage repaired and the building restored to its original appearance in order to preserve its unique outward style of architecture.

The Point of Rocks station still exists and is in active railroad service. Traffic is heavy at

POINT OF ROCKS, MARYLAND. The tower of the station is a prominent feature, with the entire tower portion from base to roof featuring different window styles. *Courtesy of the Maryland Historical Trust.*

POINT OF ROCKS, MARYLAND. Rear-corner view looking toward the express office and back waiting-room area on May 12, 1969. Note that the track elevation in the foreground is slightly higher than the tracks on the other side of the station where the walkway at left slopes down to it. *C. L. Andrews Photo.*

POINT OF ROCKS, MARYLAND. The Point of Rocks station as it looked in February 1970, still displaying its most interesting Victorian Gothic Revival style of architecture. The station is a most imposing structure in Point of Rocks and a landmark there for over one hundred years. *Herbert H. Harwood, Jr.*

the station with commuter train service, and it is here, too, that helper units are put on to eastbound freights. The sophisticated architecture of the station in its rural setting makes it the most imposing building in Point of Rocks. The building easily ranks with others of the Victorian Gothic Revival, and continues to survive as a functioning station of the railroad. The station is now listed on the National Register of Historic Places, with verification dated 1973.

Rockville, Maryland

The Rockville station is located in Montgomery County, Maryland, on the Baltimore and Ohio main line east of Washington, DC. The station was built in 1873 by the Baltimore and Ohio Railroad and is one of the few B & O picturesque country stations still surviving.

As part of the development of the B & O's Metropolitan Branch, the erection of the Rockville station was important to the growth of the town of Rockville. When the Rockville station opened on May 19, 1873, the population of the town was less than seven hundred persons, but by 1890 the population had more than doubled this figure. The Rockville staton facility was easily accessible to Washington, DC, by way of passenger trains that then provided cheap and efficient transportation between these two points. After the opening of the Rockville station, the town became an attractive and close place for hotel accommodations, and Rockville soon enjoyed popularity as a summer resort. The station was also a transfer point for passengers departing to Brookeville, Olney, and Sandy Spring by way of private conveyance for the completion of their journey. As many as three grand hotels were in Rockville at the time, a significant number then for a small town. A small, freight house next to the station added to the town's business. Horse-drawn carriages brought many of Washington's prominent residents from the station to the hotels in their country atmosphere and setting.

The two-story station building is of a Victorian and Eastlake style—especially in its gables. The structure is basically of red-brick construction with a projected right-angled gable central bay, flanked on both sides by wings that make up the major axis. The roof of the longest axis is gabled and hipped at the ends, and there are dormers flanking the central bay, having a similar design to it but on a smaller scale. Arched supported brackets are under the hipped gabled ends and are more pointed in the dormers and central bay section. The roof sections were originally of slate shingles laid in light and dark bands, and two short chimneys on the roof peak flanked the central bay gable roof where it intersects the longest axis.

Windows of the second-floor dormers and bay have pointed arches in the Gothic style, as do the first-floor windows. Windows of the first and second floors and gables have alternated stone-hood voussoir blocks, the windows of the first floor being longer and narrower in style. Three bands of light-colored courses run along the exterior walls at the base just below the first-floor window sills, above the voussoirs of the bay windows, and just below the sills of the end gable windows. A decorative motif of brickwork spans the central-gable facade just

ROCKVILLE, MARYLAND. The B & O Rockville station as it looked in 1917. The station has not changed much since it was built in 1873. Note the smaller freight building at right and the wooden planked platforms on both sides of the tracks. The automobile parked at extreme left in this view might be considered an antique today. *The Montgomery County Historical Society, Inc.*

ROCKVILLE, MARYLAND. The end and rear portion of the station showing roof dormers, the central extension at left, and small canopy cover over the inner walkway, as it looked in 1954. *The Montgomery County Historical Society, Inc.*

ROCKVILLE, MARYLAND. Rockville station is on the B & O main line east of Washington, DC, and is the first B & O station west of Point of Rocks. This view of June 1972 shows the building's modified Gothic design and alternate colored roof pattern that still existed along with its old wood-planked platform. *Herbert H. Harwood, Jr.*

above and below the window sill. In the gabled-wall section and that of the dormers, the walls have board-and-batten finish painted fawn with rust color on the trimmings, including the dormer window architraves, and both colors are used in the twin doors of the first floor. The rear of the building has a wing at right angles to the main longitudinal axis, with a decorative dormer window. Flanking the front trackside bay, just below the dormer windows on either side, are plain shelter roofs braced at intervals and having black, rolled roofing. Eaves run across the fronts of these overhangs to down spouts at the central bay, and there is a single hanging-light fixture centered over the door locations under each of these overhangs. A wide, wood, slightly raised platform spans the front of the station with two long, wood steps adjoining it and set slightly back from the tracks.

Today, the Rockville station is still used as a station stop for commuters on two daily trains. The building is still owned by the B & O and is presently used as headquarters for the Veterans of Foreign Wars local chapter. It was placed on the National Register of Historic Places, with verification dated 1974. The station has deteriorated over the years, but not seriously. A rapid-transit system will eventually be coming to Rockville following the rail line of the B & O. This will necessitate the moving of the station building some 35 feet, and at the same time it will be turned around to face the street. It is hoped that when the station is moved the B & O may turn it over to the City of Rockville, which will refurbish it, but its future use has not yet been determined.

The more than one-hundred-year-old Rockville station is significant for its role in the early development of the town and for its architecture, being one of the few remaining nineteenth-century B & O stations still in use today.

Salem, Oregon

The Southern Pacific's station at Salem was located fifty-three miles south of Portland on the Portland-Eugene main line in central Oregon. The ornate wood-frame building was built originally as a passenger station in 1896 and was the second of three stations at Salem. The original station was built by the Oregon and California Railroad, now Southern Pacific, and was located about two miles away from the second station site.

The accompanying photographs show the 1896 station at three different periods: in 1896 when it was built, in 1900, and in 1913—just five years before it was replaced by the presently existing station.

The 1896 view shows the station as it was originally built—very elegant and with much attention to detail and ornamentation. The building was one and a half stories, originally 21 by 46 feet, with a porte cochere opposite the railroad tracks. A large, gabled roof with decorative ridging covered the main section of the building, with the first-floor exterior covered with wide tongue-and-groove horizontal siding. Wide, rectangular, multipaned windows covered most of the wall on the first floor rear side from which slender, carved, round columns supported the projecting porte cochere. On one end of the building was a small, baggage room projecting only a short distance, with separate attached hipped roof. The other main portion of the building on the first floor was occupied by passenger facilities, including waiting rooms and ticket office. The slight roof overhangs were supported by carved decorative brackets, including the porte cochere and baggage room overhangs. The main roof also had one broad, triangular, attic dormer opposite the baggage room end that projected from the main sloping roof. The roof of the porte cochere had twin petite-gable designs between which was a single window of the second floor. All roof peaks were topped with the same ornate-styled ridging, and a single decorative brick chimney was located on the main roof just slightly off-center next to the ridging. Small twin balconies flanked the bay window of the second floor at trackside, with a shorter roof projection over the first-floor bay window. Windows on this side and one end of the building had multipaned upper sash and twin-paned movable lower sash. Both gables of the second floor had wood-shingled siding in identical patterns that contrasted well in the overall siding style.

As the early 1896 photo view shows, platforms had not yet been installed around the building, and it is believed that this view was taken shortly after the station opened for service. In addition to the train-passenger service, a single rail line at the rear of the station served passenger traffic to and from the town of Salem

SALEM, OREGON. Southern Pacific's Salem station in 1896. This is the second of three stations at Salem; the first, built by the Oregon and California Railroad (now Southern Pacific), was about two miles away. Small horse-drawn rail cars carried people to and from the station. *Southern Pacific.*

SALEM, OREGON. A northbound train waits at Salem station in this photo from 1900 when horse-drawn wagons and buggies carried freight and people to and from the station. The freight portion had been added to the original portion of the station. *Southern Pacific.*

SALEM, OREGON. A trackside view of Salem station in 1913. The open, covered, waiting area seen at right was an addition not seen in the other earlier views. Note the old automobile and portion of a coach wagon at right. *Southern Pacific.*

SALEM, OREGON. A 1913 rear view of the Salem station, showing a door addition to the left of the freight room door at the corner, end wall. A Wells Fargo Express freight wagon is seen at left. The style of the additions has been maintained with that of the original portion of the structure. *Southern Pacific.*

by the Salem Street Railway Company. Passengers could use this modern conveyance to and from the station as an alternate to stage coaches and other horse-drawn vehicles also pictured in the 1896 view. The Salem Street Railway line to the station was then one line that entered from one point, stopped at the station, and continued along the same line to the original departure point. The street railway cars were horse-drawn, quaint little four-wheel vehicles with street names painted on a panel across the upper frames of the side windows. Branch lines of the street railway also joined to the single line to the station.

As rail traffic increased, a large, freight room extension was added a few years later to the original baggage-room end of the building, as seen in the view taken in 1900. The general design and style of the building was retained with this new addition that included wide, freight doors on the side walls, each having a single row of multipaned lights. The end had a set of twin high-placed windows and a lower set of small, sliding, baggage doors. The roof was of the same style, with braced overhang and same designed roof ridging. The view of 1900 also shows that no extension had been made at the time to the opposite end of the building.

In 1913, an extension to the opposite end had been made, as evident in the 1913 trackside photograph. An open waiting area with columned supported roof extension was added to conform in style with the rest of the building's architecture. A new entry door at the freight end of the station was also added, as can be seen in the 1913 rear view. Again the design and style of the station's architecture was retained in an effective, harmonious manner for the overall appearance of the building.

The Salem station continued in service until 1918 when it was retired. It was replaced that same year by a larger brick station building immediately adjacent to the site of the 1896 station which is still in use today, housing district freight offices, agent's office, and Amtrak facilities. The older 1896 Salem station was an excellent example of railroad-station architecture. Though it lasted only twenty-two years before it was retired, the revisions made to it well illustrated the ingenuity of the changes and additions that can be implemented in an existing structure while still retaining a fine harmonious blending of alterations that result in a most handsome station building.

San Juan Capistrano, California

The San Juan Capistrano station is located in Orange County in southern California, 57.6 miles south of Los Angeles on the Atchison, Topeka, and Santa Fe Railroad's Los Angeles to San Diego Surf Line. The station was built in 1895 by the Santa Fe Railroad and is of the California Mission-Revival style of architecture.

The station originally contained three rooms that included a passenger waiting room, an office, and a baggage room. The building is somewhat of an L-shaped structure, one story high with a two-story bell tower located at the intersection of the two wings, both of which contain open colonnaded platform areas, one of which faces trackside. The building is basically of brick construction with stucco finish that has long since peeled off from most surface wall areas, exposing the brick construction. The roofs of the two wings are of red Spanish tiles that terminate at the eave lines. The tower roof is domed and topped with a small decorative extension on which is mounted a plain weather vane. The rear of the station building had a small, auto parking space, and at trackside is a long, paved, ground-level platform that extends on either side of the building. At the north end of this platform and some two hundred feet from the station building is a smaller plain, single-story freight house having an elevated freight platform.

Windows and doors of the main station building are rectangular, set deep, and have very shallow arches with one-over-one sash windows, each having four lights. A narrow, decorative brick trim surrounds the building just under the eave line line of the wings and around the tower's square base which is built slightly higher. There are four decorative pieces mounted one at each corner of the upper, wide, tower base, their pointed tips long since broken off, and the small part of the tower projects up from this wider base, with beveled corners, creating a modified octagonal design that continues in the domed tower roof. There are four open arched windows, one on each side wall, with petite, stepped brick ornnamnted design on both the inner widths at the commencement of the arched base line. A decorative frieze also surrounds the tower, separating the walls from the commencement of the dome base.

There was some landscaping at the tower end of the building and shrubbery that added a contrast to the white finish of the building. Station name signs were painted on the upper outer walls, and the name "Santa Fe Route" once appeared along the upper tower main

SAN JUAN CAPISTRANO, CALIFORNIA. An early view of the San Juan Capistrano station taken about ten years after it was built in 1895. Note the bell in the tower, the name painted as Santa Fe Route, and the freight house at left. The railing fence along the track at right no longer exists. *Atchison, Topeka and Santa Fe.*

SAN JUAN CAPISTRANO, CALIFORNIA. A view of the station just after it was closed in 1968. Much of the brickwork is evident in this view at the colonade area and tower, with stucco on the walls at extreme left. *Santa Fe Railway.*

SAN JUAN CAPISTRANO, CALIFORNIA. The station originally contained an office, a waiting room, and a baggage room. The open colonade area is on two sides, both meeting the corner tower. This view shows the rear area and part of a parking lot as it looked on August 12, 1968. *Henry E. Bender, Jr.*

SAN JUAN CAPISTRANO, CALIFORNIA. The trackside view of the station and freight house as it was on November 4, 1972. The station was converted into a Depot Restaurant complex and the freight house to a bar and lounge area. This view shows the station and freight house prior to their conversions. *Henry E. Bender, Jr. E. Bender, Jr.*

152

base under the frieze but has long since been whitewashed over.

The San Juan Capistrano station continued in operation until 1968 when service was discontinued and the building closed. In 1974, the Santa Fe Industries, Incorporated, through its subsidiary, the Santa Fe Land Improvement Company, had negotiated a long-term lease with the Eureka and Eel River Railway Company, Inc. that would permit the station to be converted into a restaurant complex. Plans for the main station building called for it to serve as a restaurant, with the open colonnade areas to be glassed in so as to provide a total accommodation for 106 guests. The existing freight house is to be converted into a bar and lounge area. The space between the main building and the freight house is to be connected by a glassed-in, overhanging, platform canopy, leaving the space along track side open to the view of passing trains. A small kitchen structure to be built behind the trackside wing of the station is to have access to a refrigerated railroad car used as a walk-in freezer. Along the other side of the trackside, overhang, platform canopy (that joins the main station building and freight house on the parking lot side away from the tracks), several railroad cars are to be located. These include a box car for rest rooms, a pullman car for a lounge and shop, another box car for staff use and offices, and a caboose converted into a retail shop.

The newly-named Capistrano Depot Restaurant complex has since been completed and opened for business on February 9, 1975. The old station building continues in its new role, and, with the alterations, one can still detect some of its original character, though much of its originality was lost in the conversion. It should be noted here that the term California Mission-Revival style is used in name only, as the railroads using this or the Spanish-Revival style did not intend to duplicate exactly all the detailed architectural features of such original buildings but wanted to create a pleasing style of building suitable for the climate and related in some way to the influence of such original styles.

All the photo views presented here show the San Juan Capistrano station as it looked prior to its conversion, thus revealing the original setting and character that it once had as a passenger-station facility.

Shawnee, Oklahoma

The Shawnee depot is located in Pottawatomie County, 39.9 miles east of Oklahoma City, and was built by the Santa Fe Railway in 1902-03 on land purchased from a railroad right of way in 1896 by John Beard at a time when this was still Oklahoma Territory. The line was eventually extended south to Pauls Valley to provide for an alternate, primary, north-south mainline route thirty miles to the west, the south portion of which was recently abandoned.

The Shawnee depot is a striking example of the Romanesque Revival of the late nineteenth century with its colonnade of curved arches, circular ticket office, and the significant battlemented tower that dominates the structure and is its most outstanding feature. The architect of the depot is unknown but is believed to have been influenced by the works of H. H. Richardson, one of the first important exponents of the late-nineteenth-century Romanesque Revival. Other similar Santa Fe depots of this design once existed in the southwest, but Shawnee is believed to be the last to survive and still be in service.

Shawnee depot is built of cut red sandstone, with an overall north-south length of 110 feet. Exterior fetures are the medieval, crenellated watchtower, steep hip roof, corbel-stepped gables, the Romanesque colonnades of curved arches, domed, circular ticket office, and red-tiled roof. Interior features are the main waiting room, 28 by 48 feet, with its high-vaulted ceiling, wood paneling, and old-style benches with arm rests between each space, and the adjacent ticket office with its south bay 20 by 28 feet, a freight room, and other smaller rooms.

The medieval-designed watchtower is perhaps the main feature of the depot and certainly one that would attract attention. It, together with the corbel-stepped gables and sandstone, gives the entire structure a rugged and sturdy appearance and perhaps was even considered a safe haven in the early days while that small western frontier town was developing. The 1908 photograph shows the depot as it was about five years after it was built.

The Santa Fe's railroad lines were busiest during the Greater Seminole oil boom in the 1920s. Just prior to that, in 1916, Pancho Villa was threatening to enter Texas, and United States troops were sent south to build up General Pershing's forces there. One troop train loaded with soldiers stopped at Shawnee, and it is said that this was the railroad's role in the social development of the small town, where soldiers and townspeople visited each other. An interesting story is told of a friendly dog called Santa Fe Bo, who apparently developed a curiosity about train travel. He would appear at the Shawnee station and wait for a train, then hobo his way on the train to

SHAWNEE, OKLAHOMA. Locomotive No. 2308, built by Brooks in 1881, stopped at Shawnee depot with her crew and a few of the local citizens to pose for this photo taken in 1908, about five years after the depot was built. The building looks much the same today as it did then. *Santa Fe Railway.*

SHAWNEE, OKLAHOMA. Shawnee depot on May 23, 1969. The building is one of the last of its style and design still in use today. The medieval tower is an outstanding feature of the depot, as well as the heavy cut stone used in the overall construction. *William F. Rapp, Jr.*

SHAWNEE, OKLAHOMA. A frontal view showing the colonade and domed, circular ticket office. The railway still maintains freight offices in part of the building. *William F. Rapp, Jr.*

some unknown destination. He would always return on another train stopping at Shawnee, get off, and repeat the adventure. One day he got confused by a noisy carload of sheep and accidentally lost a leg under a train wheel. But once healed, he continued his daily adventures on three legs. Santa Fe Bo died of old age and was buried near the tracks with a proper headstone marker that trainmen still keep clear of weeds to this day.

As passenger train service declined, the depot was used for freight service only. The building is still generally sound in construction but in need of extensive repairs and maintenance. The depot is still occupied in part by the Atchison, Topeka and Santa Fe Railway Company, which has freight offices there. The railway has offered the city of Shawnee a ninety-nine-year lease on the building with the condition of furnishing comparable-sized office quarters to take the place of the present offices in the station building. The Pottawatomie County Historical Society hopes to have the use of the station. Should this society occupy it, it plans to make the depot its Bicentennial project. This project would involve restoration of the station, using the waiting room and ticket office for museum purposes, and converting the freight room into a crafts room for six Indian tribes, namely the Shawnee, Seminole, Kickapoo, Sac, Fox, and the Pottawatomie of this area.

Shawnee depot is significant because of its role in the town's early development, as a depot in preserved significance, and as a depot designed in the classic sense. It was fully utilized in the past with facilities for the public, unlike smaller replacement depots that are compact and lack facilities for public use. The Shawnee depot is on the National Register of Historic Places, verification dated 1974, and was declared a National Landmark recently.

Somerville, New Jersey

SOMERVILLE, NEW JERSEY. The Somerville station as it looked in the early 1920s before alterations were made to the building and tracks relocated. Note that the broad-arched entries are still open next to the tower. The station looks much the same in this view as when it was built. *Courtesy Warren B. Crater.*

SOMERVILLE, NEW JERSEY. A general view facing trackside, showing the various roof levels and window styles. This side is the same one seen in the 1920s view, except it shows the open-shelter extension at right that was added. *Tom Kelcec Photo.*

The Somerville station is located twenty-eight miles west of Newark in New Jersey at the junction of the Somerville-Flemington branch line and Newark-Hampton main line of the Central Railroad of New Jersey. The station was built for the railroad in the 1880s from a design by architect Frank V. Bodine of Asbury Park, New Jersey. Construction was done under the direction of the railroad's superintendent, William H. Peddle.

The solid appearance of the station is evident from the use of light-grey, cut sandstone in the basic construction. The building is one story in the main portion, with a two-story central section and corner tower. Some alterations and additions have been made to the building, though it remains basically much the same today as when originally built. The station has several interesting architectural features that include a porte cochere, tower, carved bracings, various window styles, and various roof levels and styles.

The second-floor roof, at right angles to the building's major axis, is hipped at streetside and rounded at trackside with a single stone chimney at center. Except for the two lower wings and tower roof, all other roof portions have patterned ridging, including the one small dormer located on the end roof next to the tower. The outer, exposed walls of the second-floor section are covered in patterned, shingled siding in contrast with the stone construction. Windows and doors of the first floor and tower are deep set, with lighter-colored stone used in the base sills and lintels, the arched windows, and doorways. There is also a light course, around the entire station about midway up the walls of the first floor, which is interrupted by doors and windows. Joined here are the bases of the same light-color stone work in the arched windows and doorways. The porte cochere has been altered since originally built, and it no longer is a porte cochere as such; the original underpass was sliced off at the first set of slender round columns closest to the building and the end roof formed into a gable and boarded in. This is clearly seen in one of the photo views where the tower and dormer are also seen in that trackside view. Similiar rounded columns, both set on stone pillars, support the roof overhang, forming an open sheltered area on one end of the building opposite the tower end. At one time, an additional porte cochere, not indicated in the old original drawings, was added at trackside between the tower and second-story section. this addition is in keeping with the general design in its stone wall and roof style.

SOMERVILLE, NEW JERSEY. A trackside view, showing roof detail and siding style used on the second-floor exterior walls. Note the lower-floor window at left was closed in. The added shelter extension is seen directly at center. *Tom Kelcec Photo.*

SOMERVILLE, NEW JERSEY. Portion of the trackside elevation, showing new walks and pavement. The second-floor shingles contrast with the heavier cut stone of the lower floor. *Tom Kelcec Photo.*

SOMERVILLE, NEW JERSEY. A portion of the station showing the main trackside entry that had been covered with a porte cochere that was a later addition. *Tom Kelcec Photo.*

160

SOMERVILLE, NEW JERSEY. A detailed view showing the massiveness of the solid cut-stone construction and arches of the entry. Note the slate roofing and deep setting of the windows and doors. *Tom Kelcec Photo.*

SOMERVILLE, NEW JERSEY. An end view of the extension overhang shelter supported by paired columns. The style of the second-floor roof is more evident here. *Tom Kelcec Photo.*

SOMERVILLE, NEW JERSEY. An overall end view showing the tower and end entry. The bell-shaped tower roof is an outstanding feature. Flower boxes occupy the lower-tower window sills. *Tom Kelcec Photo.*

SOMERVILLE, NEW JERSEY. A streetside view of the station as it looked in October 1975. Note that the original roof cresting is still intact, even on the small dormer. This same dormer is seen in the 1920s view, and by comparison one can see where the end of the projecting roof overhang has been cut and boarded in, as seen in this view. *Tom Kelcec Photo.*

SOMERVILLE, NEW JERSEY. A fullside view facing away from the currently existing tracks located on the opposite side behind the station. Note the eyelet roof vent and the boarded-in windows of the second floor. *Tom Kelcec Photo.*

SOMERVILLE, NEW JERSEY. A general view from the relocated trackside with the station at left. The tracks had been elevated and open platform shelters installed, as seen in this October 1975 view. *Tom Kelcec Photo.*

The building originally contained on the first floor a general waiting room, smoking room, ladies' room, and ticket and telegraph room in the tower area. Also toilet rooms and a baggage room were at the end of the building opposite the tower end. Steps next to the baggage room led up to the second-floor rooms that were used mainly as offices. The building had a steam-heating system and electric lights.

A wood platform once surrounded the building at both ends of trackside and at the porte-cochere area. This has long since been replaced with poured concrete and curbed. In 1926, the tracks were relocated on an upgrade away from the station building and new, canopied shelters erected on both sides of the tracks over island platforms reached by foot subway from the station.

The station still retains much of its original character, with its contrasting stone-and-black-slate roof. The window frames, doors, and dormer windows are painted green with a lighter, now faded, cream color in the door panels and window trims. The eaves are green, as are the small, round column bases and wood bracings. The second-story exterior walls are white, and all the roof ridging is outlined in orange.

The Somerville station still exists and is a stop for commuter trains, and the station building is still used at this writing. The building is a fine example of late-nineteenth-century railroad-station architecture executed in cut stone. Though some minor repairs and painting are needed, the structure is worthy of preservaton for its historic association with the town of Somerville and for its most interesting style of architecture.

Stoughton, Massachusetts

The Stoughton railroad station, located in Norfolk County, Massachusetts, facing east on Wyman Street and one block from the town's main street, was originally built for the Boston and Providence Railroad, and later acquired by the New York, New Haven and Hartford Railroad. The substantially built station building was designed in 1888 by Charles Brigham of Sturgis & Brigham, architects of Boston, Massachusetts. The station is of local importance as Stoughton's most significant public building linked historically to the development of local industry and as a style of late-nineteenth-century railroad architecture that remains basically unaltered and in excellent condition.

The building is constructed of rough-hewn granite with slate roofing and with an imposing square, clock tower that rises above the main building at that time would qualify it as a head-station.

The station itself has overall dimensions of 88 by about 66 feet. The clock tower, with its large circular dials, is 15 feet square and 62 feet high, and is situated on the northeast end of the building. Narrow, light-emitting, lancet windows are in stepped positions on the central position of the tower walls. There is a porte cochere, originally used as a carriage porch, at the north of the tower, which is covered by a hip roof and supported by four granite piers.

There is also a pedimental portico at the entrance on the same side of the building as the tower. On the west side is a wooden, covered platform running perpendicularly to the station on that side. Windows contrast in design from arched, lancet, and rectangular-shaped (as used for the women's waiting room and ticket office. All roof peaks of the main building have decorative ridging.

The main building has a rectangular, men's waiting room, telegraph office, and baggage room at the north end, with a twelve-sided, women's waiting room at the south end, giving a circular-shaped effect at the end of the building. The ticket office is centrally located, with windows on three sides facing the interior men's and women's waiting rooms. The men's and women's waiting rooms have their own fireplace and separate stone chimney. The interior is substantially finished in hardwood, with pine floors so as to create a most pleasing appearance for all who entered this outstanding building.

In addition to its local importance, Stoughton station is also of state-wide importance because of its early involvement in the expansion of the railroad to the southeastern part of the state. In the last third of the nineteenth century, many stations in more important locations had towers that were considered vital elements to the design and impressiveness

STOUGHTON, MASSACHUSETTS. An early engraving of the Stoughton station that had been used by various railroads over the years. The station looks much the same today as it does in this view. *Courtesy Massachusetts Bay Transportation Authority.*

STOUGHTON, MASSACHUSETTS. A July 1970 view of Stoughton station that is still currently in use now by the Metropolitan Boston Transportation Authority. The station was placed on the National Register of Historic Places in 1974. Note the date and station name set in the triangular space of the roof overhang at right. *Herbert H. Harwood, Jr. Photo, C. L. Andrews Collection.*

STOUGHTON, MASSACHUSETTS. Stoughton station is considered one of the most significant buildings in Stoughton. It continues to be in service and excellent condition, as seen in this photo of July 1970. The square tower is a dominant feature of the building with its stepped narrow windows and inset clock faces. *Herbert H. Harwood, Jr.*

of buildings of distinction for the community in which the railroad station was a major part. The Stoughton station is now unique for its design, since it is the only remaining towered station of the Classical-Revival style built by the railroad during the late-nineteenth and early-twentieth centuries in this state. The design, by Charles Brigham, now being recognized for his role in the Classical-Revival style of architecture, is a most significant one of national architectural importance in relation to other similar buildings built by him.

Stoughton station is currently owned by the Metropolitan Boston Transportation Authority and is still in use for transportation service. The building remains on its original site in good condition and was placed on the National Register of Historic Places, with verification dated 1974.

Strafford, Pennsylvania

STRAFFORD, PENNSYLVANIA. The Strafford depot as it originally looked when known and located at Wayne, Pennsylvania, in 1885-86 before it was moved. Note that the building once had a basement level or sublevel on which it rested, with wide steps leading up from a planked platform at trackside. Much of the original roof cresting no longer exists, although the basic exterior wall design remains intact. *Courtesy Newton K. Gregg.*

STRAFFORD, PENNSYLVANIA. A June 1975 view of the Strafford station as it looked prior to repainting in July and August of that same year. The station was first used as a railroad station by the Pennsylvania Railroad between 1885 and 1886, when it was located at Wayne, Pennsylvania, at which time it was a single-story structure, the lower floor being added when it was relocated permanently at Strafford. *Herbert H. Harwood, Jr.*

SOMERVILLE, NEW JERSEY. A street-side view of the Somerville station taken in October 1975. The sturdy architecture of the building still remains intact, retaining much of its original design and character, although some alterations had been made to it over the years. Commuter trains still stop at the shelters on the upgraded tracks, which were relocated in 1926, and the main station building is still in use today. *Thomas Kelcec.*

STRAFFORD, PENNSYLVANIA. The Strafford depot as it exists today with its additions and alterations. The covered stairway at lower right leads down to the lower-level parking lot. The front open porch is also an addition. *Herbert H. Harwood, Jr.*

The Strafford depot is perhaps one of the most interesting little depots in North America—for its architecture, and also for its interesting background. It is unique; there is only one of its kind. Although there is some question as to the validity of the building's early background history prior to 1885, there is a framed document posted under glass inside the depot that gives the following account of its origin and its present location.

"The Stafford depot building was a single-story structure originally constructed in Japan, then shipped to Fairmount Park in Philadelphia, where it was assembled by Japanese workmen and first used as the Japanese pavilion during the 1876 American Centennial. Later it was used as the Illinois State pavilion. Subsequently it was moved to Wayne, Pennsylvania, located 0.9 miles east of Strafford, and used here for the first time as a railroad depot between 1885-86. Its location as a depot building at Wayne is verified, and the building as it originally existed at that time is seen in the 1885 photo view presented here. It was then moved west from Wayne towards Strafford and used as a railroad depot at the location known as Eagle, Pennsylvania. It was at the Eagle site briefly and then again moved to the present Stafford, Pennsylvania, location in 1887. Since its beginning use as a railroad depot in 1885, it served the Pennsylvania Railroad."

The portion of this account that is questioned is its origin and its use as the Japanese pavilion in Fairmount Park and as the Illinois State pavilion. Old books and catalogs on the Centennial Exposition indicate that neither the Japanese pavilion nor the Illinois State pavilion building had the slightest resemblance to the depot building. It is quite possible its

STRAFFORD, PENNSYLVANIA. The rear lower level showing the building's full lower-floor addition and the stairway at left that leads up to the long trackside platform. All the major additions were made when the depot was moved and installed at this site. *Herbert H. Harwood, Jr.*

STRAFFORD, PENNSYLVANIA. A general trackside view taken September 1975, showing the long narrow platform fronting four sets of tracks. *Charles M. Smith.*

170

STRAFFORD, PENNSYLVANIA. The upper trackside level, showing the open-canopy waiting area with benches and the center entry door with the covered stairway to the lower level at right. *Charles M. Smith.*

origin and use as a pavilion may be valid and that the illustrations published in these early works of the Japanese and Illinois State pavilions may have been done before this structure was set in place there or after it had been removed. In any case, there appears to be no valid record of its origin unless the document posted inside the Strafford depot now is accepted.

When the depot building was relocated at the Strafford site in 1887, it was given additions and some revisions to allow for the two-level position it now occupies. At trackside the ground level slopes back from the depot's platform down to a lower level where an automobile parking lot now exists. The lower level required the major addition of a lower story to the original building, with the original, main, first-floor portion on a level with the upper-track grade. Other additions included an open, platform canopy attached to the original main building portion at trackside. A long wood-planked platform was also added along trackside, and at one end of the depot connecting to the platform, two flights of canopy-covered steps led down to the lower-grade level of the parking lot. Some other alterations made at various times include a new roof, revised and new chimneys, removal of ornate trimmings on the roof, platform-lighting additions, and more recently, in 1975, a new painting of the building

Strafford is on the Philadelphia-Pittsburgh main line of the Pennsylvania Railroad, now

171

STRAFFORD, PENNSYLVANIA. An end view of the depot taken September 1975, showing both the upper and lower levels. The electrified wires of the railroad can be seen at right spanning the tracks. *Charles M. Smith.*

STRAFFORD, PENNSYLVANIA. A partial end view next to the covered stairway, showing detail of the wall panels and gable with intricate designs and twin narrow-arched windows. *Charles M. Smith.*

STRAFFORD, PENNSYLVANIA. A partial rear view showing the bay projection and dormer with their wide overhanging roofs of similar design. *Charles M. Smith.*

STRAFFORD, PENNSYLVANIA. The trackside gable, showing carvings in triangled panels, and carved brackets, with the top of the entry door in the background. *Charles M. Smith.*

STRAFFORD, PENNSYLVANIA. A close-up view of the carved bracings and trackside shelter-roof support timbers. These additions match the original building well. *Charles M. Smith.*

STRAFFORD, PENNSYLVANIA. Detail of the trackside entry door with hand-grip railings. Note the style of the wood bench at lower right. *Charles M. Smith.*

Penn Central. This line was electrified from Philadelphia to Paolie in 1914, and through to Harrisburg in 1938. Electric motive power is used for both freight and passenger service, and trains stopping at Strafford are usually made up of electric MU cars.

The depot contains a waiting room and an office. A partition between the two does not go all the way to the ceiling. There are also rest rooms off the waiting room, which accounts for the overhang on the south side. When the depot was repainted, a job that stretched out through July and August, 1975 the body of the building was painted cream and the trim a very dark green. The depot was badly in need of painting, and apparently these colors are the same shades as the ones used previously, though it was thought from the more weathered places that the trim may have been brown at one time.

The Strafford depot is still existing and in active service for the Penn Central Railroad, being used by seventy weekday trains, fifty-eight Saturday trains, and thirty-six Sunday trains. An agent is on duty weekdays, and the little building, unique in its still-visible ornate style of architecture, is now a well-kept suburban depot and still offers service after one hundred years' existence.

Timber, Oregon

TIMBER, OREGON. A rare view of Southern Pacific's depot at Timber, Oregon, under construction in the Summer of 1915. The railway tracks at left were installed first along the line passing the depot site. Additional tracks were installed after the depot was completed that same year. Note that the stone chimney, windows, and doors are not yet completed. *Southern Pacific*.

Timber depot was built by the Southern Pacific Railroad and was located on what is now known as the Southern Pacific's Tillamook Branch. This line was undertaken in 1905-06 by the Pacific Railway & Navigation Company under the direction of E. E. Lytle. It was opened for through traffic between Hillsboro and Tillamook on January 1, 1912. Progressively from the east, the line continued from Hillsboro to Buxton by 1906, and on to Wedeburg in 1909. From the west, the line was built from Tillamook to Mohler prior to 1911, with operations through to Mohler on July 17, 1911. During the 1910-11 period, all operations, freight and passenger, were on construction trains. The line was completed from Wedeburg to Mohler in the 1909-11 period. The work was extensive and involved eleven tunnels and heavy, canyon construction. Southern Pacific acquired the line on July 1, 1915, the same year the Timber, Oregon, depot was constructed.

Timber is about at the summit of the Tillamook line from Portland amidst forests and a great logging industry that developed. At that time the village of Timber consisted of only a few homes, a post office, and a grocery store; these were the beginnings of a town that would soon develop with the coming of the railroad. The depot at Timber was an important place for the village, as were many old depots built in the West when small towns began to grow and prosper as new railway lines progressed.

Timber depot was located in the heart of the woods at a high elevation of the coast range

TIMBER, OREGON. The Timber depot in 1915, just after it was completed. Note that only one track line is in place, with grade being made ready for additional tracks at left with ties stacked at right. *Courtesy of Walter W. Henzi.*

TIMBER, OREGON. A small portable work-crew hut is on the freight platform and was used by those who built the station. The late 1915 view shows other newly installed tracks fronting the depot. *H. A. Arey Photo, Guy L. Dunscomb Colllection.*

TIMBER, OREGON. Looking down the line at Timber in this late 1915 view with the depot at right center. The switch track at left led down to a slightly lower grade behind the depot. *H. A. Arey Photo, Guy L. Dunscomb Collection.*

TIMBER, OREGON. A double-header passenger train has arrived at the Timber depot. The freight platform at left has steps leading up to it from the lower grade below, and the slope grade of the siding track in the foreground is evident, as seen in this 1916 view. *H. A. Arey Photo, Guy L. Dunscomb Collection.*

TIMBER, OREGON. The scene at Timber depot in the summer of 1916 when the depot was in full operation. The little depot was a busy center for the area and continued to be so until it was destroyed by fire in 1955. *H. A. Arey Photo, Guy L. Dunscomb Collection.*

TIMBER, OREGON. A portion of the forest area at Timber is seen in this scenic view of 1916. Note that the box car at right is on the lower grade-level siding on that side of the building. *H. A. Arey Photo, Guy L. Dunscomb Collection.*

TIMBER, OREGON. A wintry scene at Timber in 1916. Note the old style lamps next to the freight door. A small sign to the right and above the lamp reads: "Western Union Telegraph & Cable Messages Accepted Here." The elevation of the Timber depot above sea level is 978 feet. *H. A. Arey Photo, Guy L. Dunscomb Collection.*

TIMBER, OREGON. Looking down the line in a winter scene at Timber, Oregon. This view was taken the same day as the view showing locomotive No. 2931 with snow plow on the locomotive. *H. A. Arey Photo, Guy L. Dunscomb Collection.*

TIMBER, OREGON. The rear lower level of the depot in the grip of winter in 1917. The heavy snows have completely covered the lower siding track. The upper grade of the main lines are at right. *Courtesy of Walter W. Henzi.*

where the logging industry developed. For this reason, the depot was built of cut logs, grooved and fitted, with a log-roof framing that extended beyond one end of the building to provide for a covered, open platform with the extension of the roof. Multipaned glass windows were inset in sturdy frames on all sides of the depot. A natural-stone chimney stack was located at the center of the open, covered platform end against the building and projected through the roof. At the opposite end of the depot, an open, planked platform the width of the building was erected with a short flight of wooden steps leading down to the lower level of the ground on the rear side of the structure. The main trackside level had a planked platform that fronted the depot and extended a considerable distance beyond either end of it.

At least three sets of tracks passed the front side of the depot, with a single line branching off at one end and grading down slightly to the rear of the depot and close to it so that cars could be serviced from the small platform, the rear side of the depot being at a lower grade level than the front side. In this setting, the depot presents an interesting structure, and it continued in service for many years. In 1955, the little pioneer depot was destroyed completely by fire.

Though its presence was relatively short, the Timber depot was important to the town and its development and also to the logging industry of the area. The railroad lines are still in operation though the depot has never been replaced. It is still remembered as a representative of the opening of the rugged forest area where tall trees grew and logging trains moved back and forth along the Tillamook line, passing the little depot at Timber as they carried their products to the nation.

Vicksburg, Mississippi

VICKSBURG, MISSISSIPPI. The original wood-frame depot at Vicksburg that was replaced by the present larger, brick station. This view of March 28, 1903, shows the wood-frame building with hipped, gabled roofs and a long porch fronting the building. A lunch room was also located in this depot, as well as passenger facilities. The sign on the tilted post in the foreground reads: "Look Out For The Locomotive." The river banks have overflowed, leaving tracks partly under water. This is a typical scene, except for the flooding, of what it was like at the old Vicksburg depot long ago. *Photo: Old Court House Museum, Vicksburg, Mississippi.*

The Vicksburg station was built in 1906 and was designed by D. H. Burnham & Company of Chicago, Illinois. The Vicksburg station is also known as the Levee Street Station and is located in Warren County, Mississippi, very close to the Louisiana-Mississippi state line and adjacent to the Yazoo River Diversion Canal that branches from the nearby Mississippi River. The station was originally built for the Yazoo & Mississippi Valley Railroad, a forerunner of the old Illinois Central Railroad and for years an integral part of the Illinois Central system operated under the Y. & M.V. name. The north-south rail line through Vicksburg came into the system as the Louisville, New Orleans and Texas Railroad. It was consolidated into the Y. & M.V. under the latter name on October 24, 1892. The Y. & M.V. routes are now part of the Illinois Central Gulf, Y. & M.V. having been absorbed into the former Illinois Central on July 1, 1946. The Illinois Central Railroad merged in August 1972 with the Gulf, Mobile and Ohio Railroad to form the Illinois Central Gulf Railroad.

The station building was originally used for passenger service and once handled passenger trains on the railroad's north-south line of the Vicksburg Route Division, which, until 1959,

VICKSBURG, MISSISSIPPI. An early view of the new Vicksburg station building, taken shortly after it was built in 1906. The sign at center above the tall columns reads: "Yazoo & Mississippi R.R. Station." This station was also known as the Levee Street Station. Note that the roads have not yet been paved. *Illinois Central Gulf Railroad.*

VICKSBURG, MISSISSIPPI. A streetside view of the Vicksburg station. This station continued in active service until 1948 when passenger service ended. The building is used today as the Illinois Central Gulf Railroad's headquarters for the Mississippi Division. The station has since deteriorated considerably, though the base structure is sound. *Illinois Central Gulf Railroad.*

portions of the present Mississippi Division were called. Passenger trains on the north-south route originally operated between New Orleans, Louisville, and Memphis.

The station building is three stories high, basically of brick construction and generally rectangular in plan, about 47 by 106 feet, not including exterior porches. The first-floor interior of the building originally contained passenger-station facilities that included a central vestibule, ticket office, and stairway leading to the second floor and basement, all contained within a narrow, rectangular-area floor space with a bay window at trackside and entry door at the opposite streetside, the longer side of this interior area being at right angles to the main building axis. The north side, flanking this central area, contained a large waiting room with smaller, men's and women's toilet rooms adjoining it. Double doors on both side walls gave access to the street and trackside. Still north of this room is a self-contained baggage room with double doors on each side wall. To the south of the central area was a larger general waiting room with a smaller smoking room and women's room opposite each other at the south end. Both waiting rooms had terrazzo tile floors and open fireplaces. Double-entry doors are also located in the same positions as

183

VICKSBURG, MISSISSIPPI. A passenger train stopped at Vicksburg station, headed by the Yazoo & Mississippi Valley Railroad locomotive No. 68. The upper portion of the station is seen in the background of this early view. *Photo: Old Court House Museum, Vicksburg, Mississippi.*

in the other waiting room but with a pair of double doors flanking the south end-wall fireplace that gave access to a semicircular, roof-covered open porch.

The second floor contained a small, roadmaster's office, a large office for engineers, supervisors, and clerks on the north end, and another large office for superintendent's clerks on the south end. The north-end office was open to an east corridor that led to the stairway, the south office area, and another smaller, private, superintendent's office at the southeast corner. The third floor is mainly usable storage space.

The exterior design of the station is generally symmetrical about its shorter center axis. A domed, two-story cupola is located on the center of the main roof, with a small square platform on the first level having a door-access to it and surrounded by a low-fenced railing. The main roof slopes down on both sides to the second-floor level, and there are two identically designed dormers with arched windows and small gabled roofs. Two short wings project out from both ends of the main building on the street side only, both having gabled roofs of identical design with a semicircular window in each gabled end. The windows and the one door on

VICKSBURG, MISSISSIPPI. An end-elevation view of Vicksburg station, taken May 3, 1976, showing the open end porch, wall facade, and a portion of the shelter at left that faces trackside. *Photo: F. B. Gautier.*

these streetside walls have the same style of stone voussoirs over them, with stone sills at the windows, and this is also found on all other windows and doors. A flat roof with outer baluster railing spans the two end wing projections and is supported by six equally spaced, two-story-high columns, forming a high open arcade on this side of the building only. Five equally spaced, arched, double-doored entry doors give access to the two waiting rooms, with the central doors leading to the vestibule of the central room that separates the waiting rooms. At the larger, general waiting-room end is the semicircular open porch with spaced columns supporting a semicircular roof and spaced with baluster railings between the columns. At trackside, long, sheltered platforms on both the station side and outbound side of the tracks once existed but have been removed.

In the summer of 1919 some alterations and additions were made to the station building that included new terrazzo-tile flooring in both the waiting rooms, and new tiled flooring in the smoking room and women's room. New radiation heating was also installed in all the rooms except for the small toilet rooms.

The station continued in its role as a passenger station until rail passenger travel gradually declined. Passenger service at the Vicksburg Levee Street Station finally ended in 1948. The last vestige of passenger-train service on the north-south route was a little train that ran between Memphis, Tennessee, and Greenville, Mississippi, as late as the 1950s.

The station still exists today, though it has not been as well maintained as in former days.

VICKSBURG, MISSISSIPPI. Vicksburg station looks much the same as it did when built. Note the Illinois Central R.R. name shown above the columned entry in this May 3, 1976, view. *Photo: F. B. Gautier.*

The natural red brick is in contrast to the white of the columns, the two-story cupola on the roof, the open semicircular porch, all window framing, and other white-painted trimmings. The station is still used today as headquarters for the Illinois Central Gulf's Mississippi Division.

Warren, Pennsylvania

The Warren station is located in Warren County, in northwest Pennsylvania just north of the Allegheny River and south of the New York state line. The station building was built in 1868-69, originally on the Philadelphia and Erie Railroad, later the Pennsylvania Railroad, and now Penn Central. In the early days of rail activity at Warren, the station was very active in both passenger and freight service for three separate railroads, but in more recent times the station was used for freight-only service when it was still occupied.

The station building itself is a rectangular-shaped, two-story structure about 40 by 145 feet in plan and basically of brick construction that has been painted over. Both ends of the building's main block have extended lower roof sections that continue along the first-floor level on both sides of the main block. The south end of the building has a single-story baggage room that adds extra length to the first-floor roof at this end. The first-floor roof overhangs extend at the ends to form platform shelters and are supported by a series of columns from which are spread carved braces that connect to form arches between and along the rows of columns at both ends. The first-floor roof is hipped, while the roof over the second story is gabled, with a gabled roof section at right angles to the longer main axis. Within the gabled ends are single small circular windows. Other windows are arched and generally set in pairs with a single sill spanning them. On each side of the central bay are sets of double doors, and this pattern of windows and doors makes the main block of the building generally symmetrical about its axis. The brickwork is slightly extended at corners, between pairs of windows, and along the contours of the eave line, forming brick panels framed within the bays and gables.

At some time in the past, alterations were made to the station building that included removal of some of the brick chimneys and removal of roof-overhang brackets under the gabled end eaves, as well as other minor alterations. For a well-used station building, well over one hundred years old, the structure is still generally intact and has not changed to any great extent since it was built. Some deterioration is evident in the eave areas and roof corners, and the building is in need of other minor repairs and painting. The interior ground-floor rooms contained passenger facilities that included a centrally located ticket office joined to a corridor, two waiting rooms, one on either side of the ticket office, and the end baggage room. The second floor contained storage rooms and other rooms not related to passenger facilities.

The last passenger train from Warren station ran in 1965, and the station building was used

WARREN, PENNSYLVANIA. A 1910 view of the Warren station just over forty years after it was built. The station looks basically the same today in its architecture. *Courtesy Warren County Historical Society.*

WARREN, PENNSYLVANIA. The general setting of the Warren station as it looked on May 2, 1976. Built in 1868-69 by the Philadelphia and Erie Railroad, the station was placed on the National Register of Historic Places in 1974. *Courtesy Charles Putnam.*

WARREN, PENNSYLVANIA. A trackside view of Warren station taken November 21, 1961, when it was still in active railroad service. *Edward W. Weber.*

WARREN, PENNSYLVANIA. A general streetside view of the station, showing the lower freight-end portion as it looked in May 1976. This side is also a parking lot area—in the foreground and at right. *Charles Putnam.*

WARREN, PENNSYLVANIA. A portion of the streetside and parking-lot area at Warren station in May 1976, showing the lower canopy shelter and arched windows of the second floor, with the windows boarded up. *Charles Putnam.*

WARREN, PENNSYLVANIA. A close-up of the supporting roof-overhang columns and braces, indicating the complexity of the under-roof supporting beams and framing. Note the scale at lower right in this view of May 1976. *Charles Putnam.*

WARREN, PENNSYLVANIA. A view of the baggage weight scale located at the south wall next to the baggage-room exterior door. This early type of scale is seldom seen now. *Charles Putnam.*

WARREN, PENNSYLVANIA. Detail of the brickwork and arched windows at the central-gable portion of the station. The building is in need of repair. *John Muldoon Photo, Edward W. Weber Collection.*

WARREN, PENNSYLVANIA. Warren station as it looked in the Summer of 1972, showing the building is vacant and with windows boarded up. The last train ran from here in 1965. Restoration would make it most significant. *John Muldoon Photo, Edward W. Weber Collection.*

for a short time for freight-only service but closed later that same year. The surrounding spacious grounds at the station are now used as a parking lot for a nearby factory; this is often filled to capacity with several hundred automobiles. A park area had been planned adjacent to the station, but nothing has been done to make that plan a reality.

The station building still exists but has not been used since 1965, so that deterioration continues. The company that rents the parking space around the building had attempted to purchase it, but the sale never went through. According to Penn Central, the station is still for sale at this writing, and the local Warren County Historical Society hopes someone will purchase and restore the building which is a local landmark and important in the early development of the area in the past. The unoccupied station building was placed on the National Register of Historic Places, with verification dated 1974. The Warren station remains as a fine example of mid-nineteenth-century railroad-station architecture. Few stations from this period still survive, and it is hoped that this station will be restored and reused for some useful purpose, as many others have been, thus preserving a style of railroad-station architecture of the early post-Civil War period.
period.

Whitehall Depot, Bryn Mawr, Pennsylvania

WHITEHALL, PENNSYLVANIA. The former Whitehall depot, as it looked in November 1975, still maintains its pre-Civil War style of architecture and character of the period. This building outlived the Bryn Mawr stone station that was built nearby to replace Whitehall when the tracks were rerouted. *Bob Storks.*

The Whitehall depot was built in 1859 by the old Philadelphia and Columbia Railroad. The original route of the railroad turned south through Bryn Mawr, then called Humphreysville, just northwest of the city of Philadelphia, and a depot called Whitehall was erected on this south route on a site that is now Haverford and Glenbrook Avenues. The Pennsylvania Railroad acquired the Philadelphia and Columbia Railroad and, in 1868, decided to straighten the line from Ardmore to Rosemont in order to eliminate the long curve around Bryn Mawr. This track relocation through Bryn Mawr was completed in 1869, thus leaving the Whitehall depot no longer in use by the railroad, as tracks were also taken up from the Whitehall depot route. A new stone station had been erected in 1869 a short distance from the Whitehall depot and was called Bryn Mawr station, which then commenced to serve on the revised train route.

The Whitehall depot was not demolished and was later reused for nonrailroad service. The building is basically rectangular in shape with a two-story central portion placed at right angles to its two adjoining single-story wings. The building design is generally symmetrical about its main axis and is of wood-frame construction with a rough stone base.

The building is very attractive in its design, with horizontal siding used on both the main first-story and second-story exterior walls. Window designs on the upper floor are arched and set in arched framing. Those of the first floor are rectangular in the two wings and arched in the two opposite bays, except for those on the front first-floor wall where the fire escape is located on what may be referred to as the

WHITEHALL, PENNSYLVANIA. Upper-story detail showing the structure's ornamented trimmings and arched-louvered fire-escape door. The building is brightly painted in white, with red roofs and black eaves. *Bob Storks.*

WHITEHALL, PENNSYLVANIA. The upper streetside, taken before air conditioning and exterior lighting on the end roof eave was installed. Note the central portion's arched windows and style of roof-overhang braces. *Bob Storks.*

WHITEHALL, PENNSYLVANIA. The upper streetside, showing installed air-conditioning unit and exterior lighting fixtures on the end roof-eave portion. *Bob Storks.*

original, front, trackside elevation of the depot. At both ends of the wings, larger window areas are found that are believed to have once been doorways, possibly baggage-room double doors or single large doors. All windows, except these two end windows, have multipaned glass with one-over-one sash. The second-story gabled roof has eaves along both sides, and all roof-line overhang edges have a continuous ornate trimming not found on the lower roofs of the wings. The second-story bay has an arched-frame, louvered, exit door that opens to the small, iron, fire-escape landing from which iron steps lead down to ground level. A single, natural-red-brick chimney from one of the first-floor-wing roofs extends up next to the central, front-bay section and through the side of the second-story roof. The roofs of both wings have shallow eaves around them, ending at down spouts along the corners of the two extended bays. The roof overhangs are supported by a series of carved-wood brackets, all of similar design.

The building is positioned now on two levels. The front street level is lower so that the natural-stone-wall base is evident up to the floor-base line of the building. The opposite side of the building has its base at street level, so that no stone base is evident here. The depot is thus positioned between two roads, so that each side faces a different road.

The old depot is well over one hundred years old now but, suprisingly, still in excellent condition for its age. It is presently in use as the Bryn Mawr Hospital Thrift Shop, and the surrounding grounds are landscaped with plants and shrubbery that create a pleasing setting for

WHITEHALL, PENNSYLVANIA. Built in 1859, the former Whitehall depot still exists in excellent condition as the Bryn Mawr Hospital Thrift Shop. The steps with hand railing, at right, lead up to the upper street level. *Bob Storks*.

the picturesque building. The exterior walls are painted white, with white trim at the roof-eave line, windows, doors, roof brackets, and second-story, roof-overhang ornamentation. The roofs of both wings and the second-story roof are a contrasting red, with eaves, downspouts, fire escape, and step railings in black. Modern additions are two small air-conditioners placed one on each side in the upper windows of the wings.

The building illustrates very well the reusable capabilities of older depots still well maintained and structurally sound. The old depot continues to display its great charm and character of early railroad-depot architecture, pleasing in design and in its attractive color combinations, set in pleasant surroundings. The Whitehall depot is an excellent example of pre-Civil War railroad-station architecture that is still in active use today and has outlived the Bryn Mawr stone depot that had replaced its facilities when the track was rerouted.

Willits, California

WILLITS, CALIFORNIA. The old depot at Willits, as it looked in 1911. The crowd had gathered with a band to celebrate the first train from Fort Bragg to Willits. This depot was replaced with a new all-redwood-constructed depot that exists today. *Courtesy California Western Railroad.*

The Willits station is a significant structure in that it is the only all-redwood-constructed station still in existence in America. The station is located on the Northwestern Pacific Railroad Company's Eureka-Willits-San Francisco line, 139.5 miles north of San Francisco in Mendocino county, California. The station was used jointly by the Northwestern Pacific Railroad and California Western Railroad for rail passenger service for many years and was considered to be one of the finest stations on the line.

The California Western Railroad is famous for its rail-motor "Skunk" cars that operated on its equally famous, forty-mile Redwood Route that curved serpentlike from Fort Bragg on the Pacific coast to inland Willits, all set amidst towering, giant-redwood trees. The Northwestern Pacific Railroad had already been in operation on its north-south line, when the California Western line from Fort Bragg to Willits was completed in 1911. The first CWR passenger train, pulled by locomotive No. 5, rolled from Fort Bragg to Willits on December 19, 1911, and was photographed as it rode the new Redwood Route that residents of the area had awaited for many years.

In the following few years, the original, two-story, wood-frame depot, that had served passengers on the Northwestern Pacific, did not seem appropriate enough or fitting for the magnificent redwood surroundings. The area was quite popular with visitors, and, when the Willits to Eureka link was completed in 1915,

WILLITS, CALIFORNIA. Locomotive No. 5 pulling the first passenger train of the California Western Railroad, on its way from Fort Bragg to Willits on December 11, 1911, along the new Redwood Route. *Courtesy California Western Railroad.*

WILLITS, CALIFORNIA. California Western Railroad flat cars were converted with benches for passenger use on excursions through the Redwood Route after it was completed. *Courtesy California Western Railroad.*

WILLITS, CALIFORNIA. California Western railcar M 100 at Willits station in August 1963. The all-redwood station had replaced the older, two-story building. This (pictured) station contained a restaurant where passengers and visitors to the area could have a meal, since no diner cars were used on this route by the Northwestern Pacific or California Western trains. *Stan F. Styles.*

WILLITS, CALIFORNIA. An October 1968 view of the all-redwood Willits station that is used by both the Northwestern Pacific and California Western Railway. It is currently used mainly by freight crews of both railroads. The station is still in excellent condition and is unique in its all red-wood construction. *Henry E. Bender, Jr.*

WILLITS, CALIFRONIA. The Northwestern Pacific's freight house at Willits, located just north of the Willits station, and seen here in an October 13, 1968, view. *Henry E. Bender, Jr.*

WILLITS, CALIFORNIA. At Willits station, 150 miles north of San Francisco, passengers wait to board the "Skunk" train for Fort Bragg, while the Northwestern Pacific's Budd car is poised to make another trip north up the Eel River canyon to Eureka. Both rail tours are exciting, especially to first-time visitors to the West. *Redwood Empire Association Photo.*

more passengers passed it on the San Francisco to Seattle run, and more visitors had access to the glorious redwoods of the area. For some time Mendocino County residents felt that the old depot was too plain and typical and not sufficiently impressive for visitors to the area who might have expected something more appropriate in keeping with the landscape of the surrounding redwoods. In 1913, civic leaders had conferred with officials of the Northwestern Pacific and had agreed to remedy the problem, at which time preparations began that would result in a new station at Willits. For nearly three years the Union Lumber Company, which had operated in the area for many years, and two other logging firms of the region set aside exceptional, clear-grain redwood, free from imperfections, that would be used for the new station (where connections are made between the two railroads).

WILLITS, CALIFORNIA. A steam "Skunk" train of the California Western Railroad at the Willits station, taking on passengers for the forty-mile tour where the rails corkscrew among giant redwood trees between Willits and Fort Bragg. Willits station is seen at left in the background where a Budd railcar awaits. *Redwood Empire Association Photo.*

Work began on the new, all-redwood station, completed in 1915, and opened for traffic in 1916. It is believed that the station was designed and built by the Union Lumber Company and deeded to the Northwestern Pacific Railroad or that someone was hired by these companies to design it. But verification of this still remains a mystery since they cannot say who designed and built the station, though it was definitely not constructed by the California Western Railroad.

When the station opened in 1916, it was considered the first and only all-redwood station in existence and a fitting tribute to the world-famous, majestic redwoods of California. The picturesque station is designed in a Tyrolean style of architecture much resembling a mountain-resort lodge.

The main station building is rectangular in shape, with a large gabled roof that overhangs considerably at both ends. The front portion of the roof, facing trackside, extends out to form a covered open-platform shelter supported by redwood beams lengthwise which are held up by a series of eight large, square, redwood columns. Each end of the roof has a decorative trim with another narrow decorative carved trim running the length of the roof line just under the eaves. There is a bay window centrally located and directly above it is a flat-roofed dormer with multipaned glass windows. Heavy redwood beam supports are evident in many places with carved designed heavy support brackets at the gable ends. Adjoining the main building is another smaller building now believed used for freight service. Across the tracks from the Willits station is the long rectangular wood-frame freight house with elevated platform, indeed in strong contrast in appearance to the redwood station.

As neither the Northwestern Pacific nor California Western had dining cars on their passenger trains, the Willits station had a double service. In addition to passenger facilities, it had a fine dining room that served passengers of both railroads.

The Willits station still exists today in good condition and is still used by the California Western Railroad. The Northwestern Pacific no longer handles passengers between Willits and Eureka or south from Willits. Freight crews of both railroads use the station now, and it is still a station stop for the California Western passenger "Skunk" trains that continue to operate passenger service on the spectacular Fort Bragg to Willits Redwood Route.

Ypsilanti, Michigan

The first depot at Ypsilanti, Michigan, was built in 1837 and was a small, wood-frame depot situated on the west side of the tracks. With the coming of the railroad through Ypsilanti from Detroit in February 1838, the depot was adequate until the 1860s when it was removed. In 1864 the Michigan Central Railroad built a new and very handsome three-story, brick, station building, also referred to as the Ypsilanti Union Depot, since it had at one time also served the Lake Shore and Michigan Southern Railroad. The new Ypsilanti depot was located on the east side of the tracks and was of Victorian-style architecture. Both the Michigan Central Railroad's Chicago-Detroit main line and the old Lake Shore and Michigan Southern branch line from Ypsilanti, southwest through Pittsfield, Saline, Bridgewater, and Manchester, Michigan, to the west, used this depot. A large part of this old line had been removed many years ago, and the only part of the line that still remains is from Lenawee Junction to Clinton, Michigan.

The Ypsilanti depot, as originally built, is a striking example of railroad station architecture. The design is not unlike many of the more stately residential buildings of the period, and, if it were not for the tracks and locomotive in the 1865 photo view, one might consider it as such. In addition to the building's three floors, a noted architectural feature was the square, tower section that extended from ground level to above the main building block. The main roof was gabled at the ends, and another was at right angles to the main building axis next to and adjoining the tower at trackside. Dormers flanked the central section, and all gables had ornate wood trimmings that carried on along the bottom edge of the end-roof overhangs. The windows were rectangular, with stone sills and lintels. A platform ran along trackside, fronting and passing the depot on either end, and a short, roof-shelter overhang extended from the building above the first-floor windows, spanning the length of the building at trackside.

Just west of the depot stood a greenhouse, where the Michigan Central raised all the cut flowers that were in the dining cars on the whole Michigan Central system at the time and in the station in Detroit that used flowers for its elegant dining room and restaurant. The grounds around the Ypsilanti depot were beautifully landscaped with the word *Ypsilanti,* outlined in flowers in one huge flower bed. The depot in its setting was one of the showcases of the whole Detroit-Chicago Michigan Central main line and presented an exceedingly handsome picturesque scene.

At the turn of the present century, a detached baggage-express building was added to the building's south end, with a covered-walk canopy connecting it to the main building. This

YPSILANTI, MICHIGAN. An 1865 view of the Ypsilanti station as it originally looked about a year after it was built. The station looked much like an elegant residential mansion of the Victorian period. The building existed as shown until 1910 when a fire destroyed the upper floors and tower. *C. T. Stoner Collection.*

YPSILANTI, MICHIGAN. A 1912 view of the Ypsilanti station, showing its major revisions after the 1910 fire. It has completely changed in style from the original, although much of this lower floor and part of the original tower remain in the alterations. This design existed as shown until the fall of 1939 when the building again met disaster. *Courtesy Samuel L. Breck, Jr.*

YPSILANTI, MICHIGAN. The Ypsilanti station as it exists now and as seen in this winter view of February 8, 1976. The windows are boarded up, and the interior is badly vandalized. *John Uckley.*

YPSILANTI, MICHIGAN. A rear view of the station and baggage-express building in the winter of 1976. *John Uckley.*

YPSILANTI, MICHIGAN. A closer view of the main station building in 1976. Note the portion of the open shelter that connects to the baggage-express building, seen at right. *John Uckley.*

YPSILANTI, MICHIGAN. A general, trackside view taken from the baggage-express end. It is hoped that the building may be saved and reused in the future, but its disposition is still in doubt at this time. *John Uckley.*

addition is a single-story, hipped-roof, brick building that still exists today as does the open-walk canopy. The top of the main building's tower roof was crowned by an ornate wrought iron trimming. It is believed that this ironwork was an attraction for lightning, so it was removed about the time the baggage-express addition was made.

The third story of the main building had been used as the station agent's living quarters. In 1910 a disastrous fire at the depot destroyed this third story and upper-tower portion. Work began to rebuild the depot, revising it drastically to a single-story building with a two-story tower which was the lower portion of the original tower. The revised and altered building is seen, in the 1912 photo view, with its new roof design, though the windows are the same as on the original building. Though the altered depot was completed, making use of the original building's first floor, it no longer resembled the handsome structure it once was, losing completely its early, ornate, Victorian style.

The Michigan Central Railroad was eventually absorbed by the New York Central System. The Ypsilanti depot continued in its service until another disaster befell it. On August 10, 1939 a New York Central freight train, westbound, derailed near the depot, with several of the freight cars slamming hard into the depot. The damage was considerable and resulted in the loss of the bay window and tower, the ticket room area, and the vestibule of the baggage-express building. The depot was again remodeled and revised to its present condition as seen in the 1976 photo views. The basic building, except for the missing tower, looked much as it did after its first major alteration.

The depot still exists today, but in a sad state, with windows boarded up and its interior having been badly vandalized. Ypsilanti is still a commuter stop for a Detroit-Jackson Amtrak commuter run every weekday. The now Penn Central-owned depot has recently come to the attention of the Ypsilanti City Council, which gave approval to plans for remodeling the depot as a tourist-attracting supper club, but the railroad has, at this writing, not committed itself to selling the depot, even though the prospective owners had promised to preserve the historical aspects of the depot. In any case, the building would certainly be better off restored than in its present shabby condition. Evidently Amtrak has also expressed interest in the depot, so that either way some chance for its continued existence is possible, though not certain, at this time.

Index

Alabama Great Southern Railroad Company, 55, 56
Alabama Mountain Lake Association, 57
Allegheny River, 187
American Association for State and Local History, 93
American Centennial, 169
Ames, David, 121
Ames, Frederick, L., 119
Ames, John S. Jr., 121
Ames, Oliver, & Sons Company, 119
Ames, Senator Oliver F., 121
Amtrack, 18, 47, 52, 112, 113, 128, 149, 208
Ann Arbor Railroad, 49, 63, 67
Ashley, James, 63
Atchison, Topeka & Santa Fe, 128, 130, 150, 156

Baldwin, E., Francis, 138
Baltimore & Ohio Railroad, 85, 138, 139, 143, 145
Bassette Charles, 35
Battle Creek, Michigan, 15-16
Beard, John, 154
"Best Friend," 25, 26
Bethlehem Jaycees Terminal, 22
Bethlehem Junior Chamber of Commerce, 20
Bethlehem, Pennsylvania, 19-22
Bicentennial Commission, Durand Area, 52
Bicentennial Project, 156
"Blue Water," 54
Bodine, Frank V., 158
Boston & Maine Railroad, 114, 116, 118
Boston & Providence Railroad, 165
Bradlee, Nathaniel J., 114
Branchville, South Carolina, 23-26
Branchville Railroad Shrine and Museum, Inc., 25-26
Brass Whistle Gift Shop, 118
Brigham, Charles, 165

Bryn Mawr Hospital Thrift Shop, 196-97
Bryn Mawr, Pennsylvania, 27-30, 194
Burlington Northern, 40
Burlington Route, 40
Bundy, G.H., 31
Burnham, D.H. & Company, 182

Caboose Museum, 33
California Mission Revival, 150, 153
California Western Railroad, 199-204
Canaan, Connecticut, 31-34
Capistrano Depot Restaurant, 153
Catoctin Mountains, 138
Centennial Exposition, 169
Central New England, 31
Central Railroad of New Jersey, 19, 20, 158
Chateauesque, 79, 90, 93, 110, 113
Chatham, Massachusetts, 35-39
Chatham Railroad Company, 35, 36, 39
Chatham Railroad Museum, 38-39
Chesapeake & Ohio Canal, 138
Chicago, Burlington & Quincy Railroad, 40
Chicago, Rock Island & Pacific Railroad, 90-91
Childs, David B., 114
Cincinnati, Indianapolis, and Western Railroad, 85
"Citibank Depot Drive-Up," 93
City National Bank of Lincoln, 90
City of Rockville, 145
Classical Revival, 167
Colman, Robert, 79
Confederate Soldiers, 23
Connecticut Railroad Historical Association, 33
Connecticut Western News, 31
Connecticut Western Railroad, 31
Conrail, 84

Conway Scenic Railroad, Inc., 117-18
Cornwall & Lebanon Railroad, 79
Creston, Iowa, 40-43
Creston roundhouse, 40
Cricket Gift Shop, 124, 127

Day, R. W., 90
Department of Public Utilities, 37
Detroit, Lansing & Northern Railroad, 63
Dubuque, Iowa, 44-47
Durand, Michigan, 48-54

Eagle, Pennsylvania, 169
Eastern Railroad, 114
Eastlake style, 98, 143
Easton Branch Railroad Company, 119
Easton Historical Society, 120-22
Easton, Massachusetts, 119
Edison, Thomas Alva, 103
Edward VII, King, 98
Eldredge, Marcellus, Honorable, 35
Eliot Realty Company, 116, 118
Englehart, Louie, 68, 72
Erie Lackawanna Railway, 127
Erie Railroad, 127
Eureka & Eel River Railway Company, Inc., 153

Fairmount Park, Philadelphia, 169
Flag Stop Snack Bar, 118
Flemish style, 79
Fort Bragg, California, 198-204
Fort Payne, Alabama, 55-57
Fort Payne Iron and Coal Company, 55
Fort Payne Opera Building, 57

Galloway, Charles W., 139
Golder, Louis, 98
Gothic Revival, 27, 30, 138
Grand Trunk Railway, 48, 49, 103, 104
Grand Trunk Western, 48, 52, 106
Grant, Ulysses S., 98
Greater Seminole oil boom, 154
Greenfield Village Museum, 103
Gulf, Mobile & Ohio Railroad, 44, 182

Hamilton, John D., 64
Hamlet, North Carolina, 58-62
Hardy, Augustus L., 36
Harrison, Benjamin, President, 98
Hawks, J.D., 108
Hewitt, George W., 79
Hinds, Earnest E., 123
Historic American Building Survey, 18
Historic Bethlehem, Inc., 20, 22
Howell, Michigan, 63 67

Hudson River, 123
Hudson River Railroad, 68
Humphreysville, 194
Hurricane Agnus floods, 84
Housatonic Railroad, 31
Housatonic route, 33

Ida, Michigan, 68-74
Illinois Central Gulf Railroad, 44, 47, 182, 183, 186
Illinois Central Railroad, 44, 182, 186
Illinois State Pavilion, 169, 171

Japan, 169
Japanese Pavilion, 169, 171

Kilmer, of Canaan, 31

Ladson, South Carolina, 75-78
Lake Shore & Michigan Southern Railroad, 68-71, 73-74
Lebanon, Pennsylvania, 79-84
Lehigh Canal, 19
Lehigh River, 19
Levee Street Station, 182, 185
Levy, William, 114, 118
Liberty, Indiana, 85-89
Lincoln, Nebraska, 90-93
Livingston County Historical Society, 64, 67
Louisville & Frankfort Railroad, 134-35
Louisville & Nashville Railroad, 134, 136
Louisville, New Orleans & Texas Railroad, 182
Love, Frank, 38-39
Lytle, E. E., 175

McDonald, Findlay, 103
Mackenzie, Jimmie, 103
Mackenzie, J. U., 103
Main, William R., 39
Maine Central Railroad, 114
Maryland Court of Appeals, 138
Medford, Oregon, 94-97
Mendocino County, 199
Menlo Park, California, 98-102
Menlo Park Chamber of Commerce, 100-101
Metropolitan Boston Transportation Authority, 166-67
Metropolitan Branch, 143
Michigan Central Railroad, 15, 17, 18, 108, 111, 205, 208
Michigan Division, 103
Michigan Historical Commission, 67
Mississippi Division, 183, 186
Mississippi River, 44, 182
Moran, Herbert, 38
Mount Clemens, Michigan, 103-7

National Landmark, 156

National Register of Historic Places, 18, 26, 33, 42, 43, 54, 57, 62, 67, 84, 93, 102, 122, 142, 145, 156, 166, 167, 188, 192
Nebraska Historical Society Register, 93
New England Transportation Company, 37
New Jersey & New York Railroad, 123, 127
New Orleans & Texas Pacific Railway, 55
New York Central, 17, 18, 68, 73, 108, 208
New York Central & Hudson River Railroad, 68
New York, New Haven & Hartford Railroad, 31, 37, 119, 120, 165
Nicholson, G. B., 55
Niles, Michigan, 108-13
North Canaan, Connecticut, 31, 32
North Carolina Division, 58
North Conway Depot Company, 118
North Conway Depot Model Railroad Club, 118
North Conway, New Hampshire, 114-18
North Easton, Massachusetts, 119-22
Northwestern Pacific Railroad, 199-204

O'Bannon, Kentucky, 137
Oklahoma Territory, 154
Old Colonial Railroad, 35
Old Colony Railroad System, 119
Oradell, New Jersey, 123-27
Orange Empire Railway Museum, Inc., 128-29, 131
Orange Empire Trolley Museum, 131
Oregon & California Railroad, 146-47

Pacific Railway & Navigation Company, 175
Parker, William A., 121
Peddle, William H., 158
Penn Central, 17, 18, 31, 49, 68, 108, 173, 187, 192, 208
Pennsylvania Railroad, 27, 29, 79, 169, 171, 187, 194
Pennsylvania Railroad Construction Department, 27
Perris, California, 128-33
Perris, Fred T., 128
Pershing, General, 154
Pewee Valley, Kentucky, 134-37
Philadelphia & Columbia Railroad, 27, 194
Philadelphia & Erie Railroad, 187-88
Pinacate, 128, 131
Point of Rocks, Maryland, 138-42
Portsmouth, Great Falls & Conway Railroad, 114-15
Potomac River, 138
Pottawatomie County, 154
Pottawatomie County Historical Society, 156

Queen Anne style, 98

Railway Express Agency, 47, 118
Ramona Pagent, 128-29
Rauch Hotel, 68
Raylrode-Daze festival, 26
Redwood Route, 199, 200, 204

Reed, Carroll P., 114, 118
Richardson, Henry H., 119-21, 154
Riddle House, 94
Robel Frocks, Inc., 80, 84
Rockville, Maryland, 143-45
Rockville station, 143, 145
Rogers & McFarlane, architects, 15, 17
Romanesque style, 79, 122, 154
Roosevelt, Teddy, 19
Ross, Raymond, R., 89

Salem, Oregon, 146-49
Salem Street Railway Company, 149
Salvin, Mathias, 36
San Francisco & San Jose Railroad, 98
San Francisco Peninsula, 102
San Juan Capistrano, California, 150-53
Santa Fe Bo, 154, 156
Santa Fe Industries, Inc., 153
Santa Fe Land Improvement Company, 153
Santa Fe Railway, 130-31, 150, 154
Santa Fe Route, 133, 150-51
Seaboard Air Line Railroad, 58, 62
Seaboard Coast Line Railroad, 62
Shawnee, Oklahoma, 154-56
Shortridge, Frank, 58
Shovel Works, 119
Shunk, Chief Engineer, 31
"Skunk" cars, rail motor, 199, 200, 202-3
Smith's Creek, Michigan, 103
Smith, Dwight, 118
Somerville, New Jersey, 157-64
Snyder, Richard, 33
South Carolina Railway, 23, 75, 76
Southern California Railway, 128, 130
Southern Michigan Railroad, 68
Southern Pacific, 94, 96-98, 100, 102, 146-47, 174-75
Southern Railway, 23, 26, 55, 56, 75
Spanish Revival style, 153
Spier and Rohns, architects, 49
Stanford, Leland, Governor of California, U.S. Senator, 98
State Historic Preservation Plan, 102
State Historical Site, 34
Station Museum, 33
Stoughton, Massachusetts, 165-67
Strafford, Pennsylvania, 168-73
Sturgis and Brigham, architects, 165
Summerville, Dorchester County, 75

Taylor, Charles, C., 55
Temecula Canyon, 128
Tillamook Branch, 175, 180
Timber, Oregon, 174-80
Toledo, Ann Arbor & Northern Michigan Railway, 48, 63
Tornblom, Ronald H., 90
Tyrolean style, 203

Union Depot, 31-32
Union Lumber Company, 202-3
Union Soldiers, 23

Veterans of Foreign Wars, local chapter, 145
Vicksburg, Mississippi, 181-86
Vicksburg Route Division, 183
Victorian style, 19, 31, 34, 79, 98, 114, 127, 141-43, 205, 208
Villa, Pancho, 154

Wales, Prince of, 98
Warren County Historical Society, 192
Warren, Pennsylvania, 187-92
Wayne, Pennsylvania, 168-69

Wayside Inn, 68
Weekly Herald, The, 103
Wells Fargo Express Office, 125, 127, 148
Whitehall depot, 30, 193-97
Willits, California, 198-204
Wilson Brothers & Company, 27
Wilson, Joseph M., 27
Woerner, Eugene, 90
World's oldest railroad junction, 26
Wright, Will, 64

Yazoo & Mississippi Valley Railroad, 182, 184
Yazoo River Diversion Canal, 182
Ypsilanti City Council, 208
Ypsilanti, Michigan, 205-8
Ypsilanti Union Depot, 205